LoveG.E.A.R.S.

A Relationship Tool Book

Grant Edmonds

LoveG.E.A.R.S.

Copyright @ 2008
All rights reserved.
ISBN: 978-0-615-24614-7

www.GrantEdmonds.com
(Link to Amazon.com)

LOVEGEARS: A RELATIONSHIP TOOL BOOK

Contents:

1) Intro—An Honest Assessment……………..………..…7

2) 1st Gear: Labels Don't Matter, Bonds Do……………..15

3) Getting Your Oil Changed: Preventive Maintenance...22

4) 2nd Gear: Having The Clear Vision - Happiness………27

5) The Great Equation……………………………………..35

6) 3rd Gear: Identifying Needs…………………………….42

7) Needs vs. Wants/The Big Three………..............………63

8) 4th Gear: Be With A Best Friend……………………….71

9) The Bag O'Crap—Issues……………………...…………76

10) Men vs. Women………………………..……………...80

11) 5th Gear: Talk Through Your Crazy, Listen Thru Your Stupid -Communication……………………………………...87

12) Self Check Q&A-Common Questions…………………104

13) Fundamentals Revisited-One Step At A Time………...132

INTRO —AN HONEST ASSESSMENT

"In theory, it's the simplest thing—a relationship. In practice however, it's the most complex thing one could ever be a part of..."

Have you ever looked at a friend, a loved one, or even a total stranger and said to yourself, "Umm...what the heck is THAT person doing with THAT **OTHER** person?" We say it all the time. I say it all the time. Heck, I've said it about myself at times! But once you can put yourself *into* that actual relationship, then it all somehow *can* make sense.

This basic fundamental observation about relationships of the intimate kind has fascinated me since I first learned to accept that procreation is a part of life, and indeed is not "ikky". (I remember that realization hit me in the sixth grade...I was behind the curve I believe...) And since the sixteenth grade (otherwise known as my senior year of college), that fascination has turned into a full-blown mission of mine to explore.

I will be upfront about this fact—I do not possess a degree of any kind with regards to psychology, psychiatry, sociology, or counseling. Some friends and strangers alike are actually **surprised** I haven't studied these topics extensively in college, but nevertheless, that's the truth of the matter.

I tell all of the college students I speak to during my interactive relationship "seminar" LoveG.E.A.R.S.* that basically I am *them*, ten years or so years down the road, with all of the experiences that go with that fact—good, bad, and ugly. And I also tell them that if I would have known about just half the bad and ugly experiences at their age that I know now, I would have saved myself a lot of problems and a lot of therapy!

*LoveG.E.A.R.S. (Grant Edmonds interActive Relationship Show) is a show I have been hosting around the country on college campuses for the last three years and will hopefully perform for many years to come. This relationship-oriented show is a semi-comedic semi-lecture involving interactive games for the students. There is a Dating Game, a Couples Game, some communication demonstrations, audience Q& A and more. But the focus of the show revolves around teaching the students methods of self-discovery. It's a humorous and fun way to teach students aspects of life that they can use every day for the rest of their lives.

While I am exaggerating (a touch) with the therapy comment, the point is, I am **not** going to pretend I'm something I'm not, like some other "experts" tend to do. Throughout this book I will continue to lay down the truth, as I see it, and be fair about it. (I'm guessing that's what you want to read about as well, huh?) Honesty with the self, after all, is the first step with everything in life. But I'll get to that point a couple chapters from now...

To continue with my honesty...I'm not going to pretend I'm perfect. I've made my share of mistakes. And frankly, I'm glad I made them. I know so much more now then I would have had I *not* stumbled at times along the way.

(And I probably would not be writing this book either) I have been in relationships that were amazing in some ways, and unhealthy in others. I have also been happily **and** unhappily engaged, married, and divorced all with the same person. I have been to the "edge of the chasm" as I like to say and found my way back. It's all been very exciting, agonizing, wonderful, stressful, uplifting, humbling, loving, heartbreaking, and most of all, one amazingly evolutionary period of growth for me.

But enough about me for now...

In relationships, we all must take the bad with the good. We have no choice. A lot of us don't want to deal with the bad stuff, which is why many of us stay single, remain in unhealthy situations, or cannot hold a long-term relationship. But dealing with the negatives is actually a *good* thing. There is so much to learn about life and yourself this way, including what works and doesn't work for you in a relationship. I always say that the only failure in life has nothing to do with making mistakes or doing something wrong, it's in the ***repeating*** of the mistakes and not learning from your errors in the first place. And yes, I have repeated a mistake or two, but overall, I've learned from my mistakes pretty quickly. But in every case, I have come out the other side a stronger and wiser person each time.

One more honest statement regarding this book...if you are primarily looking for a step-by-step set of directions to dating successfully, or how to be the most romantic person on the planet, or the best way to get laid, you may be disappointed between this set of covers. None of those things are my focus here.

Yet, the topics I *do* discuss should definitely *help* you in all of those areas…just perhaps not in the way you're expecting. My focus in this book is helping you to find the right person for you in a long-term relationship.

Finally, I also am not going to pretend I understand every situation, and every problem in all relationships. So, I'm not going to hand you every answer. And it's not for a lack of caring or trying, it's just the reality of things. And I can't change reality (believe me I've tried that too).

Part of that reality as to why any of us cannot know the answer to relationships all of the time is due to Relationship Law #1: *Every relationship is different and unique.* No two relationships are the same. No two people are the same, so no two people together would be the same, right? Every combination of energy and personalities are unique.

There may be similarities, but you will never experience the same exact experience of love with each passing relationship. And if you feel you have, you probably haven't been exploring your relationships hard enough. There are always differences. Now, when you're *outside* of the "dynamics" of a relationship, it becomes even more difficult to provide the perfect answer to a problem. So I repeat, I am not an expert…at least not regarding your or anyone else's life. Just on mine.

Relationship Law #2: *You* all are experts on your own lives. Or at least, you should be. No one knows you better than you, and that includes me, your counselor, your friends, and your family.

"So what are you saying Grant? If you are not an expert…how are you really helping me more than anyone else can?"

Fair question.

Aside from my life experiences, and of course the topic of who I am personally, there is only one thing that I can contribute "expertise" on. Or at least only one thing of which I believe I possess a very solid grasp.

The Fundamentals.

The fundamentals of relationships. Sounds pretty basic, obvious, and simple. That's the thing…they should be. But even if we know these fundamentals, we tend to forget them in relationships, or at least forget how to use them within the parameters of a relationship. The fundamentals are what I use to help you, and anyone I've ever talked to (including myself), fulfill individual and relationship potential. I provide the tools for you to build with. Or to put it more accurately, show *you* how to find *your* tools and put them to use in the most productive fashion you can in your relationship life. It's all about maximizing your potential.

Think of your favorite sports team for instance (preferably one that's good). It doesn't matter what sport. That team has a particular type of game plan. That team has a particular set of strengths and weaknesses. That team has a certain way to "win the game". Just like you. Will they always win? No. Just like you.

But their "game plan", or "team personality" if you will, is not necessarily better than another team's. Different, yes. Just like the differences between you and everyone else you encounter. Your personality is different from everyone else's. Thus, you will "win over" a partner in a different way than anyone else will "win over" their partner. Again, it may be similar…but it won't be *exactly* the same. You need to use your gifts appropriately, just like your favorite sports team does (hopefully).

Sticking with the sports theme a bit longer, it's the team that has the best grasp of the *fundamentals* of the sport that **always** puts itself in the best position to win. It's the sloppy team that tends to waste the talent they have, resulting in unproductive and often losing seasons. Baseball teams normally don't win the World Series if they commit many errors. Basketball teams normally don't win games having a high turnover ratio. Good fundamentals will eliminate many mistakes.

My favorite analogy currently is in the game of football. Look at the New England Patriots. Throughout the 2000's they have not been the most talented team in the league (well, except possibly for their 2007 season where they ironically lost). They have won 3 Super Bowls as of this writing, and I dare say they could have easily won another couple had a couple of things bounced their way. Regardless of how much their Spygate tendencies may or may not have influenced their success, there is no denying that their grasp of fundamentals of the game of football the first half of this decade was second-to-none. I have rarely seen them unprepared and unfocused.

On the flipside, look at the Cincinnati Bengals. Talent galore, but only **one** season over .500 the last five seasons? Is there a team more unfocused and undisciplined with the fundamentals of the game than the Bengals? Not many.

For those of you who care if I'm biased or not…no, I do not tend to root for or against either one of those teams. They are not in my "love and hate" categories. But they are in my respect and disrespect categories.

My point is, the better grasp **you** have of relationship fundamentals, the better the chance you have of maximizing your potential and "winning the relationship game".

This is the main reason I talk about and emphasize fundamentals so much. Another reason is because these fundamentals **apply to everyone**. The quote at the beginning of the chapter I remember hearing as a child (unfortunately I don't remember who said it). But I have carried that on as one of my favorite quotes about relationships. It's just an ironic saying. Relationships and their issues seem simple from the outside, and in a way they are. But viewing from the outside is done without the emotional ties, the expectations, and the energy bonds. Add all of those elements into the mix however, and relationships become a different beast altogether. At least, they *seem* that way. All relationships *can* become an out-of-control monster. But all of them can also be kept fairly simple as well…like other peoples' relationships may seem to you.

My goal is to help you help yourself better than you ever thought you could. To not have you rely on outside advice all of the time and to see things for what they are.

To help you keep things simple. **To teach the fundamentals**.

I will separate the most important points of this book into Relationship Laws, or even into whole chapters—the Love "Gears"—which will contain thorough exploration of the most important relationship points to remember. These Laws and Gears contain the simple fundamentals I have learned through reading, other people, counseling, and most importantly, my personal experience. However, don't confuse "simplicity" as to mean a "lack of depth", for there will be plenty of depth within these pages.

Remember, even though it may not *seem* like it as you are reading through this, upon reflection of these words you will find your own "step-by-step" dating process, your own romantic flavor, and your own best way to have a fulfilling sex life as well.

Just stay open and honest with yourself, and it all shall reveal itself. Let's begin…

FIRST GEAR:
LABELS DON'T MATTER—BONDS DO

To paraphrase my initial question of the book…"Have you ever known anyone who is engaged or married, and you really don't know why?"

I'm guessing you have. And if you're one of those rare people who don't, I'm sure your best friend does. I'm also guessing you've had a past relationship, intimate or otherwise, where you can look back and say, "What was I thinking?" And if you still don't understand what I'm getting at, let me fill you in.

Many of our relationships fail primarily because we fail to see what the bond is in the first place. I'd venture to say at least 98% of people have had at least one relationship in their lives where the bond has been ignored or not explored to it's fullest extent, resulting in one of two things: Either the relationship is made to be "more than it is", or the relationship is "cheapened" or bypassed altogether.

For instance, the pattern I have tended to follow in my distant past is to make my friendships with women "more than they are". I have over the last ten years become much better at seeing the reality of a situation with women, but this "idealism" affected me until I got married. Sometimes I've confused a more platonic love with a physical love. I've confused the ability to be 100% myself with someone, or to have a great *chemistry* with someone, as to be in love with them.

And other times, I've confused a sexual attraction with someone to be a "relationship worthy" situation. All of these things individually are good qualities, but do not necessarily equal a wholesome and successful intimate relationship. I have skipped steps along the way, and have let logic fall by the wayside and pretended that the foundation I had with someone was stronger than it really was.

And I know I'm not even close to being alone with this personal issue.

A lot of us lie to ourselves regarding the nature of our relationship. Our hopes and ideals outweigh the **reality** of the situation. Every relationship I had in my early 20s followed that pattern. My ex-wife and I both suffered from this "affliction". No disrespect intended towards either one of us of course, but the truth of the matter was we could not "see the forest for the trees". Did we have a tight bond in some ways? Yes. Did we love each other? Yes. But our bond was tenuous in some very important areas. And because of this, I believe it was meant to end no matter what we did. We just didn't have enough "bond-wise" to sustain it. That's nothing personal towards her or myself, but the strength of our bond could only hold so much weight, even though we believed that it, along with our love, could support everything we put upon it.

For instance, I'm a huge talker and communicator in general. Not just big, but **HUGE**. My ex-wife was not. She always said to me that she'd work on her conversational skills and sometimes we actually had lengthy conversations.

But more often than not, they weren't occurring enough for me or occurring to the depths I wanted and needed. My communication needs I'm sure were all probably too much for her to deal with on a consistent basis. Nothing wrong with either one of us here, but we just had different needs.

Also, we always said we'd work on our spiritual bond throughout our relationship, but when one person believes in one thing religiously, and the other believes in something different…well, that's just the way it is. You can't change someone and their beliefs, nor should you try.

You can't "create" the bond, you can only explore and **discover** it. What we believe is what we believe, who we are conversationally is who we are. And these are two **huge** parts of anyone's being. We can't change these things without changing ourselves, or without lying to ourselves about who we are. A bond is what it is, because we are individually who we are. We need what we need, for our core being is what it is. Sure, you can try to "change" the other person, but rest assured they will **always** revert back to the way they were if they are not trying to change themselves **for themselves**. All the love in the world could not change that in my marriage, and more often than not, we'd end up frustrating the hell out of each other, so the love, unfortunately, would take a back seat. That's just what happens without a strong, solid bond.

On the other hand the problem I have *not* suffered from, because it isn't in my nature, is the one others tend to cling to quite a bit.

And that is the problem of *not exploring a bond fully, or at all.* At times, we do this because we have "been there/done that" with a certain type of person, so we don't want to "waste time" exploring someone who we know from previous experiences isn't our "type". That is perfectly understandable.

However, a problem may arise when this avoidance is due purely to insecurities or fear of the individual. This too is understandable and perfectly natural. Many people do not want the responsibility of a relationship, or do not want to make the *effort* to get to know someone. Rather, they would prefer something more superficial and/or easy to deal with.

There's nothing inherently wrong with this. But what if we are "too frightened of a good thing?" Or too afraid to deal with our deepest emotions? Or just too scared to initiate a dating process with someone who for all we know, could be **the one**. We shortchange ourselves and leave the bond unexplored. That's a shame. The trouble comes when we may accidentally "pass up" a good thing because we have failed to get to know what is really there within that person in the first place.

Most everyone primarily fits into one of these two categories. There's nothing inherently wrong with wanting badly to make a relationship work, or on the other hand, not wanting to explore a relationship fully. But when these two processes are taken to extremes, and we avoid the reality of the situation, we then end up shortchanging ourselves one way or another. Again, we all will most likely make this mistake once, twice, or even twenty times in our lives. But the first step to healing this destructive habit is to be *aware* of it. Only then can we take action to remedy it.

Which category do you fit under? The "idealizer" or the "shortchanger"? Realize it and remember it.

As far as what to do about finding what your bond is (and I'll talk about this at length later too), you need to become **very** knowledgeable about the other person. Just like you would with your best friend. See how you flow together, what your similarities are, and how you get along on a day-to-day basis. The key ingredients to finding your bond with someone is *time* and *patience*. And do it, if at all possible, *in person.* Do not rely on technology (ie. Your computer or your cell phone) for dating purposes. It's a nice ice-breaker, sure, but you will only find out so much this way. If you have to have a long-distance situation, you of course do what you can, but when you're **really** trying to get to know someone and need to see if you're compatible at the early stages of the relationship (ie. The first year) there needs to be a sufficient amount of face-to-face time. If you put in some honest effort, and go into the discovery process clear-headed and without fear, in time you will find your exact connection. Again, I will explore this further in the next few chapters.

Right now I'm going to give a perfect (and scary) example of how people confuse the actual bond they have with the label they attach to it.

You ever hear someone say, "Once we get married (or engaged), we'll be happy."? Or, "Everything will get better once I have the ring on my finger."? Beware of these comments, those are *red flags*. Remember, if the relationship is not good entering that high level of commitment—engagement or marriage- it will only get worse after that level has been reached.

Oftentimes people are not truly ready for that next level, but defiantly attach that label to themselves by proposing or getting married anyway. This is one of the biggest reasons for the high divorce rate today. People don't take the time necessary to explore a bond and therefore "jump the gun."

I understand there are many pressures, stresses, and expectations in life, and a lot of outside commitments that make it tougher to take the time needed to know someone fully enough to make that intimate commitment solid and reliable. But trust me on this one—take whatever time **you** need. Again, no two people are alike, and no two couples are alike. Some couples may know they belong together for life a lot quicker than others. That's fine, but just make sure that **you do what's right for you.** I don't care if your partner is pressuring you. You are (or should be) a team, yes, but you are still the only person responsible for **you**. Make sure your needs are met. I personally need a *lot* of time to get to know somebody to the point where I feel 100% ready to commit to them for life. I refuse to bow to any pressure to take steps before I am ready. This is even more true after my previous marriage, and I dated her for four years! I may know someone else well enough after a year or two, but in the case with my ex-wife, I think that fifth year of dating would have made a **huge** difference for us. I was *willing* to get married, but I was not quite *ready* yet…that's a big difference. Many of us follow the willingness we have, rather than the actual readiness we possess for that type of commitment. And you have to have both.

But alas, we live and learn. No regrets. It's helped me become wiser and more careful for the future.

Back to the point…the key again to knowing your bond with your partner is to take your time, and be patient. Don't force things. And be honest with yourselves. In time, the bond will reveal itself—good, bad, or ugly. (Or all three!)

Relationship Law #3: The label does not make the bond, the bond makes the label. Don't put the cart before the horse.

GETTING YOUR OIL CHANGED— PREVENTIVE MAINTENANCE

Before we go any further with more fundamental lessons, I want to stress the most important reason for reading this book.

And that is: So you can save your sanity, and maintain your overall well-being while you're in a relationship. And believe it or not, even some money.

Let me explain.

Why do you get oil changes in your car? To keep the engine running smoothly, right? You don't want the engine to fink out on you in the middle of a long trip do you? Why do you go in for physical checkups at the doctor yearly (in theory…)? To keep your body running smoothly, right? You don't want to have your heart peter out…well…ever! When early detection of high cholesterol could alert you to changing your eating and exercise habits in time to prevent a heart attack, well…it's easy to see the advantages of a check up.

So why don't we seek relationship checkups more often?

Hmm…good question…

Maybe because it's not life or death. But it sure can feel like it sometimes!

Seriously, there are two reasons I can think of for people not getting relationship check-ups. First of all, to get professional help from a couples' therapist, it costs money. Now, I will say that if you find a good therapist and can afford it, therapy is an awesome experience. I am forever in debt to my counselor (and not just in a monetary way). Everything about my marriage became clear to me through my sessions, and frankly, considering my mindset at the time, I **really** needed it. I was too far gone to take care of it by myself at that time.

The other reason people don't normally seek out professional help is that it may hurt their ego and pride. Or they worry because they believe the way others perceive them may change. They feel that they are weaker or lesser people somehow for doing so. While I understand that feeling, all I can say is…*get over it!*

Yes, get over it. If you put your pride or ego above your well-being or your partner's well-being, then I have nothing to say other than your priorities are out of whack. Truth **IS** hard to take at times, but you won't evolve and get better unless you confront it, and a counselor provides a helpful safe haven in which to do that.

Actually, some other people think that therapy just doesn't work either because they've had a bad experience, or they just don't "believe in the system." In that case…umm…find someone who's good, someone who you like and someone you have faith in. There **are** some counselors/therapists who don't connect well with certain individuals, and some who frankly just aren't that great. But overall, helping people is what they are *trained* to do, so they most likely have some knowledge you lack. So, there **are** people out there who can help.

Other than the money and the potential blow to the ego or pride one may have, I cannot fathom why one wouldn't want to get help when help is needed. Going to good friends for advice can even seem like too much of an effort at times, despite their potential helpfulness. So, without advice from counselors or friends, what does this leave for us, ideally? ***Taking care of our own issues and relationship problems by ourselves.*** And that's what the point of this book is…giving you the know-how to self-check.

Taking care of problems seems obvious and simple on the one hand. On the other, it seems like a daunting task. A lot of times we place the blame on our partner, because taking responsibility for our own deficiencies can be scary and ego-shattering. It bruises us. But that bruise will heal. Eventually it won't feel like a bruise. You have to be willing to accept the occasional bruise, because otherwise a body-crushing blow will pack quite the knockout punch later on at some point in the future.

My point is that no one wants things to "come to a head" and explode. Whether it's your car engine, your heart, or your relationship. Many times we wait until there's too much on the table to deal with. We feel we can blow off the little things. And maybe we should, but if we can't, we can't. It's much better to take care of issues as they pop up rather than let them collect. You can only keep so much stuff in a container. You can only store so much junk in the attic. Eventually, it's going to be full, and the junk will come pouring out. We all have our limits. That's something I thought I was impervious to in the past. I thought I'd let everything roll off my back, but really, every bit of crap was piling up within me, and caused me unrealized stress.

Speaking of crap...

Another way I tend to look at this "attic full of junk" is by saying we all have our "bag o' crap". It's my favorite saying, because it's the most humorous and most accurate.

I'm sure you've all heard the phrase "he/she has a lot of baggage." I just use *bag o'crap* as the term of choice. Partly because it's funny, sure, but mostly because it gets the point across effectively. The term "baggage" is not in and of itself undesirable. You could say that baggage "weighs you down", which may be true. But it's not something we tend to think of as repulsive in any way. Imagine literally holding a piece of baggage in one hand and a bag o' crap in the other. Which one would you want to get rid of first? Probably the crap. In reality, we can carry around baggage the rest of our lives, having it weigh us down...but we can find a way to deal with it. And this is probably the most accurate term to use to describe our relationship problems, because we **can** live that way, even though it's not desirable, even though it's no fun, even though it's unhealthy. But it is **possible** to do. We need to start thinking of our personal and relationship issues as "*crap*"... something we **cannot** live with. That's a much healthier way to think and live, and will more easily guide you into finding the partner you really want.

So that's why I use that terminology.

Anyway, we **can** wait until our container explodes, our baggage drags us down, or our crap putrefies until…well…fill in your own effect, (or whatever other analogy you want to use—I will use "cleaning your filter" a lot on the following pages too), but do we really want to let these undesirable things happen to us? No. We *can* let things, like our cars, or bodies, break down. But they're more difficult and more expensive to fix after they're broken.

We have to have checkups to prevent breakdowns, whether it's on our cars, our bodies, or ourselves and our relationships. You can go, and sometimes should go, to friends, family members, or counselors for help with these issues. But it's easier, cheaper, and ideal if you can do these checkups on your own, and with your partner. So, I'm going to keep digging deeper in each succeeding chapter to help you with that in the following pages…

SECOND GEAR:
HAVING THE CLEAR VISION—HAPPINESS

"Do personal issues affect a relationship?"
-A question all too often asked by students at my shows.

Answer: "Yes…in more ways than you can imagine."

In order to give yourself a "clean bill of health" during a self-checkup, you need to find your "happy place". Your happiness will play an **enormous** factor in any relationships you have.

When I ask people what they think the three main types of relationships are I usually hear something along the lines of: "Lovers, friends, and family." Sometimes I hear the reply, "romantic relationships, friendships, and mentor/student relationships." Occasionally other answers are given, but it's the absence of the most important answer by others that concerns me. The most important relationship of all is the one you have with…(drum roll please)…*yourself*.

Sounds obvious, right? Most people miss it.

Sometimes people ask me, "Grant, if you had to sum up in one sentence how to keep a relationship strong and healthy, what would you say?" I tell them, "Follow the three rules: Be yourself, love yourself, and love your partner." Notice how two of the three rules involve the word *yourself*.

That's the root of everything. And it makes loving your partner a **LOT** easier too…but I'll get to that in a bit…

You've probably heard all of the sayings and clichés: "You can't truly love someone else until you love yourself," "You can't be happy in a relationship until you're happy yourself." They are all true. The one constant in all these sayings is, again, **yourself**.

Many of the "experts" say that a lack of communication is the number one reason relationships fail. Some say it's the lack of continued romance, or a disagreement over how to handle money or kids (for the more committed couples). There are other reasons too, and yes, they all play a part. But to hit that dead horse once more, if you have a solid, happy relationship with yourself, all of these situations have a tendency to resolve themselves in a relatively stress-free way. I am not saying that there is **no** stress if the individuals involved in a relationship are stable and happy individuals. But the amount of stress is a **lot** less than it would be if the individuals were unhappy and unstable. The less stress for the individuals leads to less stress for the relationship. And who wouldn't want less stress?

One of the examples that many of you can relate to on some level comes from a certain popular TV couple. I'm guessing you are familiar with the show Friends. Ross and Rachel's 10 year on-and-off television romance was a continual hot topic among the show's fans. And while the show itself is a piece of fiction, this particular relationship felt very real on many levels.

Whether you were a fan of those two being together or not, Ross and Rachel were a prime example of the biggest issue in relationships—the lack of personal happiness. Both of these characters were doomed from the start to a short-term fate because they had a multitude of insecurities preventing them from a healthy relationship. By the end of the series, they *had* grown and evolved somewhat to a certain level of happiness and comfort. They may still not have worked (which is what I would have bet on), but the relationship's projected failure would most likely have been based on their incompatibility of their individual needs rather than their personal insecurities. I will talk more about personal needs later, but the issue here is that the constant stress of the Ross and Rachel relationship over the majority of the series was due to the fact that neither truly loved themselves yet, and hence, were not truly happy with themselves.

Point being, relationships can be really difficult to deal with if you don't have yourself in order. A lot of "control-freaks" become that way simply because they don't have themselves in order. "Control freaks" normally feel little control over their own lives. As a result, they try to "tame" their environment around them, including other people in their lives. And the people closest to them tend to suffer. This applies to any relationship—familial, friend, or romantic. But the key to a successful relationship is to **not control** the other person in any way. The more control that's exerted over another, the weaker the relationship becomes, because at least one-half of that team is not being who they are naturally, and thus the uniqueness and potency of the relationship is diluted.

So, Relationship Law #4 is: ***The less controlling the partners, the more the relationship flourishes.***

And guess what the best antidote to "controlling" a relationship is.

You guessed it: Personal happiness is the key to letting a relationship breathe.

And therefore, I believe personal happiness to be the number one reason relationships tend to succeed or fail. Personal happiness takes care of two-thirds of my successful relationship criteria: the "Being yourself" and "Loving yourself" parts.

Now, does this mean that if two individuals are very happy as individuals that the relationship is **guaranteed** to work? No, not at all. Happiness does not mean you can or should be with ***anyone.*** On the other side of the coin, if both individuals have a lot of "crap" still to deal with in their personal lives preventing them from being happy individuals, does this mean they're doomed in a relationship? Again, no. But again, it's a **LOT** easier *with* the happiness than without it. The analogy I like to use is that happiness is like having "clear vision". For instance, do you wear corrective lenses (glasses, contacts) of any kind? Would you rather **not** wear them and be unable to see clearly? Probably not. Also, do you tend to clean your car's windshield when it's full of dirt, snow, ice, or bird crap?

I'm guessing you usually do. After all, would you prefer driving **with** this stuff blocking your vision? Again, probably not. So, would you rather carry around that bag o'crap in your head clogging up your brain so you can't see things for what they are?

No?

There's the point.

As it is walking around with blurry vision, or driving around with smeared windshields, most of us tend to live life not truly seeing what's really in front of us. You *can* get to where you're going with limited vision, but it will take more time and effort than it would if you were unencumbered with these limitations.

To use the car analogy once again—The cars on the road with different degrees of "windshield cleanliness" are all seeing things differently. The cars with the cleanest windshields are normally getting where they have to go the fastest, and with the least amount of resistance. The foggy, dirty wind shielded cars are taking more time and effort to get to where they need to go. What's the one constant factor in all of this chaos?

Though everyone sees reality differently, the *reality outside is what it is*. And that ultimate reality is the same for everyone, whether they see it or not. We all tend to make our individual perceptions our reality, and then make our reality **the** reality. And thus, we believe that reality is the reality that **everyone** sees. But again, that's not how it really is.

You've all heard the tale of all the blind men using their hands to learn what an elephant looks like. One feels the tail, another touches the trunk, one the belly, etc. So they all have different ideas and descriptions for what an elephant looks like. A lot of people quit after a certain point trying to see what reality is. And if they have big ole' blinders on, or have "clogged filters", they are in trouble, for they are only seeing a piece of the bigger picture. They are only seeing the "tail" or the "trunk" of the situation. Of course, the blind men in the story could keep exploring the elephant, but it takes a lot more time and effort than if they could visibly *see* it in front of their faces.

I remember a story my mother told me before I got my contact lenses. She said that she wished she got her glasses at an early age, for she didn't even know (much less could appreciate the fact) that trees had individual leaves on their branches. She couldn't see the beauty that was a full-blooming tree. (She probably also ran into some trees on her way to school, but that's another story). Likewise, if we remove the "vision impediments" from our personal filters, we can appreciate the beauty of all of our relationships a lot more. And we can see the obstacles that stand before us and deal with them a lot quicker than someone who has a clogged personal filter.

I've brought up the term "personal filter" a few times. We all need to keep them clean, but in addition to that, we also all wear our own spiritual goggles.

We all would see the world differently even if everybody

was stable and happy. That's natural. But the cleaner our filters, the better we see reality. Our filter will never be perfect, but we need to try. No matter how close to perfect we all get, we will all perceive things a bit differently. I don't say that to discourage anyone…just as a reminder that everyone is naturally different, so don't expect others to view things the way you do. And of course, you can't change others' views…just clear up your own filter the best you can.

Relationship Law #5: *"When you cannot have a solid connection with yourself, you are not ready to have an intimate connection with another."* Work on **you** first, clean **your** slate, put on **your** corrective lenses, clean **your** filter, whatever you want to say, and when you're in a good place individually, you are truly ready for a relationship of the intimate kind. You will be open to it, trusting in it, and ready to take the healthy steps necessary to truly be intimate in every way. And in the "worst-case" scenarios, if the relationship doesn't work in the long run, you will truly be okay afterwards. Yes, you'll probably be depressed for a time, but you'll bounce back more quickly, with less emotional scars than you would have otherwise.

I realize most of us aren't always in this idealized predicament. Life gets in the way, and love comes into your life at seemingly random times. You can't always be at the top of your game. I know I haven't been. But the point of this whole diatribe is to learn to **focus on yourself** first. Because if you won't, you'll be behind the eight ball. However, as long as your *priorities* are in the proper order, and you're putting forth the *effort,* you'll be okay. Remember, in an intimate relationship (as well as the rest of life) it's the journey that's important, not the destination.

Focus on you, not on getting yourself a partner, and your chances of being successful in love greatly increases. You will find the partner of your dreams if you are fine as you are. And if you clear your vision completely along the way, more power to you!

The state of happiness is a wonderful place to be. But to **truly** be happy is easier said than done. Just watch Ross and Rachel to see how difficult that could be. But in fiction and reality there is a **huge** reason why it is so difficult to achieve. A reason many of us are not fulfilling this desire of happiness is simply because, as strange as it sounds, we really don't know how. In the next chapter I will dig even deeper and give you ideas on how to enhance the happiness in your life.

THE GREAT EQUATION

Without using the word "Happy", can you describe what happiness feels like?

Not easy, huh?

Happiness **is** hard for us to describe. And because of that, sometimes it's even harder to know exactly how to get to our "happy place".

Excuse me for pairing it down to an equation, but here it is:

Happiness=Energy=Attention

What the heck are you talking about Grant?

Well, we all know what it **feels** like to be happy, despite our struggles in defining the sensation. "Joyful, pleased, glad, content" are all words we can use to define "happy". However, true happiness goes beyond that. Hopefully you have all experienced true happiness in your lives. Whether you have or not though, I'm sure you know instinctively what happiness is on its most basic level.

Now, when I say the word "Energy"—which is defined as "the capacity for being active"—I am talking about our energy **level**. I believe we all have an energy "setting"— some of us are naturally very energetic people, some of us are not, and the rest of us are somewhere in-between. Our energy level fluctuates, but our basic setting is what it is.

And finally, the word "Attention" by definition is "paying heed" or "care" to someone or something. We all know what that is.

So, the words are well known. But this hypothetical equation is not. What I am saying with this equation is that all three of these things are interconnected on a very fundamental level.

Let's examine the first piece of the equation: Happiness equals Energy. The foundation of our happiness is based on our energy level. The energy however, is relative to each individual's natural energy setting.

Like I've stated, we all have different natural settings, or "capacity for being active", so a "high" energy level for one individual, may be a "normal" or "low" setting for another. Just like a "low" setting for one person may be a "normal" or "high" setting for someone else.

Your happiness is dependent upon where *your* energy level is, relative to your natural energy setting. So if your energy is at a high level for **you**, you will be a happier person. Simple.

You still with me?

Let me put it this way…do you have an easier time being happy when you are tired? Some of you may say yes. But you're probably thinking about that "second wind" that may kick in when you feel delirious, loopy, and what not. That too though, is an energy reserve kicking in from somewhere within you.

Others of you may say you are very happy when you are tired because you know sleep is coming and you enjoy sleeping so much.

I'll give you that one.

But when you have to be conscious and face life, being tired only makes things harder. So, let's pretend sleep is not an option here, eh? In this case, it's easier to be happy when you're awake right? Right. Okay, moving on…

The second part of the equation is: Energy equals Attention. If we are all honest with ourselves, we have to admit that we all enjoy some type of attention, right? Again, some of us more than others, but we all have *some* little need for it at least. This part of the equation simply means, "Where your attention is, energy follows."

The best way to illustrate this process is through my favorite pastime: talking. Have you ever had such an incredible conversation with someone else that you lose track of time and you leave feeling revitalized, like you could have talked with that person forever? I hope so. On the flipside, have you ever had such a horrible conversation with someone else that you left feeling drained, and probably never wanting to talk with that person again? Just for the sake of this comparison, I hope so, since it makes this point easier.

Why was the great conversation you had great? I'm just guessing here, but I'm guessing that there were probably free exchanges of ideas, interesting topics of conversation, lots of good listening in addition to the talking…the point is, for whatever reasons, you were paying **attention** to each other.

On the flipside, why was your horrible conversation so bad? Perhaps someone was hogging the conversation, maybe there were few (or no) topics of interest to you, there was probably very little listening done by one or both people, and maybe the "conversation" became more adversarial and turned into some sort of argument. In all of these cases, there is little emphasis placed on communicating. Rather, the focus is on personal ego and insecurity. You may be paying attention to the person talking to you (at least for a time), but who is **that** person paying attention to? They're just paying attention to themselves.

In some cases, they probably couldn't care less if they were talking to you, a stranger, their pet, or a wall. Many people just like to hear themselves talk. But in the cases where **you** are part of these unhealthy conversations, the attention--and hence the energy--is uni-directional. Flowing one way only. That is why you leave those conversations feeling drained. The other person essentially "sucked" the energy out of you. In the productive conversation example, both people are focusing on the other, letting the energy flow and build. Hence, the "energized" feeling you both tend to have at the end of the good conversation.

I won't go into all of the metaphysics of the situation, since I am no scientist, and I'd probably bore many of you with the details. But in essence, this is what happens. It's just my personal theory, but it hasn't failed me yet!

I want to backtrack briefly and say for the record that I myself have been guilty of **causing** the loss of others' energy at times through conversation. We probably all have

in some shape or form. Just as in the rest of this book, I write this to help you (as well as myself) be aware of what does happen in these circumstances, so we remember and can consciously change our patterns for hopes of more healthy and productive conversations in the future.
Again, I'm human and I make mistakes as well. But I must say I am a much better communicator now because I am aware of this fact and can much more easily tell when I start "hogging" a conversation. So many ineffective and unhealthy modes of communication would be remedied by the simple act of each party involved simply **paying attention** to whoever's speaking. I'll get more into that in later chapters though.

At any rate, the more attention we get, the more energy we have, and thus the happier we tend to become. (Happiness equals Energy, and Energy equals Attention, so Happiness has to equal Attention too.) But, as evidenced by the conversation examples, the more attention we get often depends on how much attention we *give.* A lot of relationships start out with us *giving* attention to each other. But many relationships then falter due to us either not giving or receiving attention from our partners. And it's probably both at the same time. Attention is a huge key in every relationship you have.

When I ask people what they like to do in general for attention, I hear everything from "talking" to "making strange faces" to "streaking down hallways". Point is, respectful or otherwise, there are millions of things one can do to get attention.

Regardless of what we do for our attention, where do we normally assume we'll receive attention from?

From *outside* of ourselves. More specifically, from *other people.*

That's all well and good. Like I said, we all have a need for at least some attention from others, even if it's just our household pets. But we **all** need a lot of attention from one person in particular—ourselves.

Again, it's about what you can do on your own here. We need to pay attention to ourselves, period. Otherwise, we start to *depend on others* for that attention, like a drug (more on that next chapter). And as a result in relationships, we tend to find our "emotions using us", as opposed to "us using our emotions." In other words, we are not in control, because we are not happy and stable. The less the outside world has an influence on us the better, and mastering your own happiness and sanity helps control your emotional reactions. You won't overreact as much to things, and will be able to keep a better balance and perspective about your relationship.

However, most of us don't know **how** to pay attention to ourselves. Thus, a lot of us don't know how to be **happy** on our own because we don't know how to pay attention to ourselves. Usually it's because we're either too lazy or too scared to do so, or we somehow think that it's "boring".

Well, I'll tell you what...if you think paying attention to yourself is boring, chances are other people will find paying attention to you boring as well. At least, you won't be as much fun as you could be to those people, and therefore will probably not draw as much attention from them as you could otherwise.

In the next chapter I will break down exactly how you can create a way to **_keep track_** of the attention you give yourself...

THIRD GEAR: IDENTIFYING YOUR NEEDS

"Be who you are, but you have to know *who* you are first…"

We've established that the number one ingredient to have in both an independent and interpersonal relationship is personal happiness. And the number one ingredient in achieving that personal happiness is receiving attention. And the best way to receive attention is…to give attention.

With yourself, (the independent relationship), **you** are in full control of the attention giving, receiving, and the happiness that comes from it. And through that happiness you experience, you are ideally prepared for any interpersonal relationship, especially of the intimate kind.

The attention you give *yourself* is the most fundamental, and most critical, ingredient to your successful relationship life. But how exactly do you pay attention to yourself?

By identifying, and then fulfilling your needs.

There are four different categories, or levels, of the "Needs Tree" as I call it. They are divided as follows: The Basic/Survival Needs, The Boundary Needs, The Value Needs, and The Honesty Needs.

Before I go on, I realize some of you may find this explanation of needs as trivial, and realize you may want to skip the rest of this chapter altogether. I wouldn't be offended if you did. But I will say that not being conscious of your everyday needs can lead to an unfulfilling personal life and relationship life. And as "together" as I thought I was through most of my life, my lack of evaluating my needs in my relationships caused **much** more drama and hardships during my 20's than I ever needed to endure. Point is, as trivial as this may seem, it's the most important set of tools I can give you for your relationship life.

Okay, now that that's out of the way…onto your individual needs.

The Basic/Survival Needs are pretty much exactly what you would envision them to be. They are what you absolutely need to survive physically, mentally, spiritually, and emotionally. To keep your body alive for instance we all need food, drink, clothing, and shelter. To keep your body *in good condition* and *happy* however we need to eat nutritious food, exercise, get physical checkups, etc. In addition, but to a significantly lesser degree, we need a certain amount of sexual activity.

Of course, there are other things I didn't list. Only you can determine exactly what you need to keep your body alive and happy. However, these *physical* needs are the most "black and white" of the basic needs, since we **all** need food, warmth, oxygen, water, etc. So most of these physical needs won't differ greatly from person to person (although the sexual need may differ).

Basic *mental* needs are more dependent on each individual. We all have a certain need to keep our mind stimulated, at least a little bit. Reading, writing, talking, listening, puzzle-solving…anything that causes you to think and use your mind is a mental necessity. Everyone has different ways of stimulating the mind, and different amounts of stimulation they need regarding these mental tasks. What are yours? Write these down if you have to.

Spiritual needs are more abstract. I divide these into the "religious" and the "creative" categories. Many of us have a certain need for connection with a higher power or with some sort of "greater good". Whether we meditate, pray, go to church or other place of worship, do good deeds and charity for others…it's all part of our spiritual needs. As for the *creative* part…most of us have a desire for something a little more abstract, a little more "grey" if you will. Dancing, acting, painting, drawing, writing, playing an instrument, or just listening to musical instruments…these are all examples of our creative spiritual needs. Again, what they are to everyone will differ from person to person. Some of us may have very little use for anything spiritual, and others may have a need for just about everything I mentioned. Again, it may be a good idea to write these down for yourself.

Finally, the *emotional* needs—otherwise known as the "need to be loved". Feeling support and care from someone is extremely important for our well-being.

All of these needs can definitely be fulfilled through others, but that is not what I am focused on right now. The point of this chapter is that **all of these needs you have can be fulfilled by you yourself.**

But I'm sure you may be dubious as to how to fulfill these needs independently of others, and may even wonder about the value of fulfilling some of these needs on your own…

"The need to talk by yourself…what's that all about?"

Yes, this is a bit different, and talking is potentially very productive with another person. But are you telling me that you don't ever talk to yourself? Or are you telling me that there is no point in talking to yourself? I beg to differ. I'm not trying to turn everyone into a bunch of crazy loons out there, but I know for my part, talking to myself helps me organize my thoughts very well. Sometimes I can talk myself through things **much** easier than I can think through them. And I will include writing (as in a journal), a means of talking to yourself. *Anything where the thoughts take physical form through words.* But I must admit I like the talking. Of course, there is a time and a place to do stuff like that, but it is quite helpful. No disrespect intended, but I believe that if you *don't* do that somehow you're either not very interesting as an individual, or you're lying to yourself…so get over it and get comfortable with vocalizing to yourself.

"How about the listening then?"

Well, I hope you're listening to yourself while you talk, otherwise yeah, you are pointlessly talking to yourself and you are one step closer to the funny farm! Of course, you can listen to yourself **think** too, and even listen to what you're **feeling**. So, even if you still refuse to vocalize thoughts to yourself, you still have much listening that you can do…

"What exactly does loving yourself entail?"

The ability to love yourself combines a few basic needs together. A lot of it has to do with faith and staying optimistic (spiritual), and maintaining confidence in yourself as well (mental). Because yes, we are not always going to be happy from moment to moment, no matter what our natural state of being. We are going to have tough times in life. But it's during the tough times when we see *exactly* what we are made of and how much we love ourselves. During the tough times is when we turn to our faith, our optimism, our confidence. But we can, and should, love ourselves before we are able to have a truly healthy relationship with another.

"Okay then…how about my sexual needs?"

There are ways to channel sexual energies into other areas. Exercising works for me, and many other people I know. I find that for me (not surprisingly), *talking* does the trick. I can personally change my sexual needs into a mental one by transferring that energy elsewhere. Odd, I know, but I can refocus that if need be. Simply because my biggest need I have with another person, or even myself, is mental stimulation. I rarely get enough of that, so that's what I do.

And of course, if none of this works, you can always fulfill your sexual energies by yourself--having "special time" as a former girlfriend of mine used to say. Of course, that depends on your values and comfort level. But rest assured it is perfectly healthy, as well as educational for your future interactive sexual endeavors. But that's enough about that.

So, we all have our individual needs, but as I brought up somewhat in the last couple pages, the ***amounts*** that we each need in each category is very different. So, we all have different ***values*** and ***limits*** we attribute to each of our needs. I'll talk about the Value Needs first. Take two people who need to exercise for example. One person may need to work out 3 times a week for an hour to feel physically "right" (I'll call this person "3")…another person may need 6 exercise sessions a week for two hours a day to feel good (I'll call this person "6"). Regardless of whether this is the social norm or whether it truly is the best way for these people to exercise, this is what they feel they need to be physically happy. And in this case, that's what matters.

To go on a tangent for a second, yes, the needs of anyone may indeed change in time, but whatever your needs are for the present moment is what ultimately matters. And yes, maybe you can delude yourselves into thinking you need more of something than you really do, but living up to your ***ideals at the moment*** is what determines your happiness.

(I will get to the issue of "wants" vs. "needs" later).
Back to the example though…let's say that "3" and "6" truly cannot be happy without their specific workout regiments. "3" and "6" **value** exercise differently. Neither is right or wrong. I should say rather that neither is right or wrong from anyone else's point of view. Because both "3" and "6" are right *for themselves.* If they are not right, happiness will not ensue, and the needs will have to be reassessed, which is okay and quite common. But as of now, "6"'s Bar is much higher than "3"'s. If "6" worked out only as much as "3" for example, he or she would not be happy. They each have their own set of values for this particular need.

The examples of differing values are endless. The *amount* you like to read, watch TV, pray, eat, listen to tunes, etc. is different than your best friend's. And no two people value everything the same…that's what makes us all unique. But the point is to **find your value for your needs**. If by exercising four times a week you are happier than when you work out three times, do it! If a year down the road, you are happier going back to three, do it! Needs do change, depending on where your life is taking you, and depending on how you change as an individual. After all, you can't do everything…

…which leads me to the third category of needs—the Boundary Needs. It's the flipside of our values. No matter how much we may value something in life, there is a limit. Have you ever played the Sims games? You know the "happy bars" at the bottom of the screen for your Sim character? (Energy, Hygiene, Comfort, Fun, Bladder, etc.) These bars need to be filled up (or emptied in regards to the Bladder bar), in order to keep them happy. But there is a limit to those bars. Just like the Sims, our bars aren't infinite. If "3" worked out like "6", he/she would probably get burnt out and turned off of the whole exercise thing. Plus, working out like "6" would mean 6 hours of eliminating something else from "3"'s life…six hours possibly devoted to another need.

Think of something you love to do. Now think of something *else* you love to do. If you spent twice as long doing the first love as you are accustomed to, what would that do to your second love? Hopefully nothing, but chances are, your time and effort spent on your second love would decrease.

At the very least, you're cutting out *something* from your life. How would that feel? I know I feel a little "off-kilter" even during my free time when I don't get enough time to listen to my music for example and instead spend more time watching TV. As far as my work goes, I don't feel quite right if I don't adequately prepare for my shows, or I don't plan my travels far enough in advance. In other words, I have to fulfill my "check list" so I can perform up to my potential each and every show. Everyone has their system, according to their needs.

We all need to know "when to say when". We need to balance all of our needs the best we can in order to be happy, and there's no way to do it if we don't put a limit on them. It is a compromise. We may value many things to an extreme degree, but we need to prioritize.

We need to know when to put a cap on those things so we can get maximum enjoyment from life and our potential happiness. I know plenty of people who love so many things, but don't discipline themselves enough to know when to stop. Often, they feel empty, or "down". And I know people who have succumbed to sicknesses quite often, or have a pattern of switching jobs often, or can't hold a relationship, all because they can't find a proper balance and put limits on their activities. I have had boundary issues myself, especially in relationships. So my tendency in the past has been to "overstay my welcome" with people and my intimate relationships. (I hope it's something that I've since remedied…)

But the most important category of needs—the Needs Tree *roots* if you will—is the Honesty Need. We all have a need to be honest with ourselves if no one else. I said that sometimes we confuse the word "want" with "need". We have to be honest with ourselves and differentiate between what is truly important to us (the needs) versus what is merely wished for (the wants). More on that topic next chapter.

We also have to be honest with ourselves and have the courage to look within at all times because our needs will *change* throughout our lives. Sometimes we assume the pattern we've **been** living is the pattern we'll **continue** to live for a long period of time. That's far from the truth. You've always heard that "the only constant in life is change." And that is a theorem that has yet to be proven wrong in the thousands of years of mankind's existence.

Therefore, you have to assume that **you** are going to change. And thusly, so will your needs. Even if it's miniscule, you will change. You need to be honest with yourself, and keep tabs on these changes as you move on through life.

This is all easier said than done I know. But this is part of the self-checking process. We need to establish some sort of pattern so we can take personal inventory of our lives—weekly, monthly, yearly, whatever. To be realistic, a yearly checkup should be doable for everyone. Maybe that should be part of a New Year's Resolution. In fact, instead of making a statement of what we want to change for the upcoming year (and forgetting all about that statement by January 3rd), we should write down a list of our Basic Needs, prioritize them, and write down our limits. Kind of a "Life Needs' Budget Plan". I guarantee you that by writing down who we are at the present moment, we will reflect on ourselves and change way more than just by stating our one goal for the year.

Unfortunately, a lot of us fear ourselves. We don't always like looking into the past. It's not always full of rainbows and lollipops and donuts (or whatever good images you'd care to create). There can be a plethora of dark places and other crap in there. But we have to acknowledge them. Not dwell on them, but acknowledge them. If we are still in a dark place, that will be reflected in our needs. And **that's okay!** Your needs are what they are. Again, you don't have to tell anyone else, and you don't have to "expose" yourself to anyone else. But the key is to become comfortable with what your needs are, and hence, **who** you are.

When that happens, you will no longer feel "exposed", and others will love you so much more easily, just as you are, imperfections and all.

But you have to know your needs. Don't be afraid of yourself.

I still have friends to this day who move job-to-job, relationship-to-relationship, without any particular direction. Often repeating the same mistakes they made previously. Why? They didn't access what their needs were, or are aware of the current ones. It's great to have goals, and I don't think anyone will ever criticize anyone else who has them. But it's even ***more*** important to know who you are now. You **can** get just about any job, any girl, any guy, etc. that you want, but you have to know what your strengths and weaknesses are, what makes you happy, and what doesn't make you happy in order to really attain what you're meant to attain. In other words--at the risk of beating the horse beyond dead--know your needs. Be honest about what they are, or you will likely not have anything "honest" come your way, be it a job, or a boyfriend or girlfriend.

Remember, knowing your needs is an ongoing process. Like I said, you change all the time, and at different rates than other people. You will find what you need through a wide variety of things in life—school subjects, extracurricular activities, your family, your friends, your work, total strangers, and most especially, your intimate relationships. I have not found anything that illuminates personal needs more so than dealing with an intimate relationship. In fact, I would say it's a *necessary* part of everyone's personal development and awareness of self.

Also remember, **don't** expect to be perfect in the assessment of your needs, especially at a young age. It's an ideal to aspire to, but like I've said before, the biggest thing is that you are *focused* on yourself and *aware* of yourself more than anything else in your life. Because you are the only one who can fulfill your needs constantly and permanently. Others will not always be around, and you do not want to become dependent on anyone else for that reason if no other. But this is what I mean when I say *pay attention* to yourself. Find your needs, focus on them, and fulfill them. If this is accomplished, everything else in life will be **much** easier to handle.

One particular scenario I see around me all of the time is the case of the "rebound scenario". This happens **way** more than people realize. We normally think of a rebound relationship as a "quick-fix" situation—someone we date, etc. just to fill a temporary void after a break up. However, many of us tend to unknowingly rebound for longer durations than that, and rebound with people who we genuinely **love** as well. Any time we are depending on someone else to **heal** us somehow in a relationship, we are still not truly ready for a healthy relationship, and hence, it is still termed a "rebound scenario".

We all must heal from previous relationships as best we can, otherwise there is a lack of clarity and balance in the current or future ones. Bad habits and negative emotions may still be ingrained in you if you have not taken sufficient time and energy to heal, and the possibility of passing these habits and emotions onto your new partner and relationship is very high. You are not doing anybody any favors this way. Anytime you are relying or depending on another **more** than yourself to heal your pain, you are being ***dependent*** and not paying enough attention to yourself. And you're basically shooting yourself in the foot in your current relationship.

If your current partner is willing to help and communicate with you about this, that's great, but you still must work through it and solve the problems independently. Writing in a diary and spending time on my own truly helped me when I went through such "rebound scenarios" in the past. Again, we will all enter these scenarios in less than ideal fashion, but be aware when you do it, so you can refocus your energies on yourself without affecting your current or future relationship.

So, we've established that you can and should fulfill all of your individual needs on your own. Now I will take identifying your personal needs to the next level. There are **also** personal needs everyone has in relationships with ***others,*** intimate or otherwise.

This is not to be confused with "Everyone needs to **be IN** a relationship". A self-made purgatory is created with that attitude. Again, if we fulfill our individual needs, we won't feel this "neediness". Relationship Law #6: ***Fulfill your needs yourself to avoid being needy—ie.***

Depending on others for your needs. Neediness overrides ***any*** good intentions. It makes smart people seem stupid, good people seem bad, sane people seem crazy. Simply because there is a desperation there. So, no one should ever feel a ***need*** to be in a relationship (more on that in a sec).

However, if we ***are*** in a relationship, there are things we need while we are in it. We all serve a purpose for each other. Every friend or girlfriend/boyfriend you have ever had served some sort of purpose in your life, as you did in theirs. Ask yourself: What **was** that purpose in each relationship? What specific things did you **need** in those relationships? And what needs went **unfulfilled**? If you can answer these questions, you can find patterns and answers regarding some of your needs. Every relationship after all, should teach you something, right? Right.

This all seems so easy on paper, but why do people remain in relationships where their daily needs go unfulfilled? To use a food analogy, if we are starving for attention, then we aren't picky about our partner and our interpersonal needs. So we settle.

However, if our "attention bars" are full, we are then picky with our partner and naturally get what we need.

Too often with our relationships, we focus more on our love for the other person than on our own needs. We sacrifice things we hold dear for the chance to achieve a "connection" or "bond" with someone. We are disrespecting ourselves when we do this.

We are not loving ourselves, or maintaining a bond with ourselves when we do this. Again, we are not paying attention to ourselves enough. *It's very important to maintain a certain independence and pay attention to ourselves a good amount even while in a relationship.*

But of course, doing the opposite can easily become a habit, and we become scared of what leaving a relationship might do to us. We are ultimately scared of ourselves at that point (or maybe of what our partner might do, but remember, that's not your responsibility). People who are "scared of themselves" are often drawn to each other. And often in these cases, one person tries to manipulate the other person, who in turn becomes comfortable being manipulated. This is why many relationships turn into abusive ones, whether it's emotional, spiritual, or physical. And those relationships are **never** healthy.

Therefore, that desperation we feel for another's attention stems from a fear we have of ourselves. We need to confront ourselves and that fear, otherwise, we will never have a truly happy and ideal relationship with another. We have to start somewhere, and it's usually best at square one. *Find a way to be happy on your own. Find a way to fulfill your needs on your own.* When you can do this, you are ready to find the right person. It's much better to be alone than be with someone who isn't right for you.

Remember, **every day in your life you are with the wrong person is a day in your life you could have met the right one.**

See why I keep repetitively preaching about focusing on your needs?

Again, I challenge you to all come up with a list of needs for yourself (the personal ones), ***and*** a list of needs you have in a relationship (the interpersonal ones). Name just a few basic needs that you have in every category, and determine exactly ***how much*** you need of each one. Here are some of my relationship needs for example (with reasons attached)-- Mentally, and emotionally, I need someone who makes an effort to truly understand me, and I need someone who can provide solid mental stimulation at the drop of a hat (ie. Lots of intelligent talking). Talking helps my mind stay active and I learn a lot that way. Plus, on a more primal level, I find conversational ability very sexy in a woman. Also, for emotional and spiritual reasons, I need a strong woman who's willing to be vulnerable. I cannot have someone who is helpless nor someone on the other end of the spectrum who is "walled-off" to me. I don't have that kind of energy and time anymore to spend digging through to the core of someone's being. I have a need for a free flow of emotions, but not someone who is unstable with them. Spiritually, she has to have a sense of humor and fun, because I am an entertainer, and am fulfilled spiritually when I laugh or I make someone around me laugh. Hence, I need a happy, stable, independent woman who can talk a lot!

I have a smaller group of needs as well that feed into those larger ones. For instance, emotionally, she needs to be supportive, but challenging and motivating at the same time. Mentally, she must be at least fairly intelligent, especially for the conversational aspect. Spiritually, she has to have a sense of a higher self, because of my need for someone optimistic and confident. And physically, as long as there is an attraction of some sort, primarily in my attraction to her face and eyes, I'm happy.

Sexual chemistry is an important need too, but so much of that for me is based on the deeper attributes of an individual; it isn't by any means purely physical. That is a big group of needs, I agree (some might call it high-maintenance), but I've found that I cannot have a long-term relationship with someone who does not have these qualities.

Ultimately, I need a true teammate who "gets" me and who doesn't play games or try to control me. Someone who can just **be**. I'm a free spirit, so I need someone who can at least somewhat identify with that.

See how the categories I mentioned for you to go over individually are also the same categories you examine in a relationship? In your intimate relationships, what are your physical, mental, spiritual, and emotional needs from another person? How much stimulation do you need in each of these areas? What are your limits in each of these areas? And how honest can you be about them?

Also, do you see how taking care of your own needs makes things so much easier in an intimate relationship? Of course, you need someone else to talk to (there's a whole different dynamic of mental stimulation when you talk to another person versus you talking to yourself after all) but when that person is gone, can you mentally stimulate yourself? Can you still entertain yourself? Can you still **pay attention** to yourself? When your significant other is gone, can you still *love* yourself? If you can, this takes so much pressure off the other person in the situation and they are freer to just **be**. As are you. And these are the healthiest of relationships. The best relationships I have witnessed include people who pay attention to themselves as much as they do to their partners. There needs to be a good balance.

There is one more point I want to cover before I wrap up this chapter. That point is the topic of rejection. The feeling of rejection is a natural, human, emotional reaction to getting "dumped", or even just not being given proper attention or consideration at a specific point in time by your partner. I've been there, and I'm sure all of you have been as well. What I am about to say may not relieve any past, present, or future *pain* of rejection, but it will definitely help you see it differently and may help you move through that feeling more quickly.

Many of us feel rejection so deeply because we take it personally. But think about it. Is rejection, of any sort, really personal? We are all different and we are who we are. Everyone's needs are different. If you don't fit someone else's needs, that's **not** a reflection on you. Rather, it's a reflection on the connection or bond the two people share, which honestly, you can't do much about.

Remember, **the bond is what it is.** You are who you are at this particular time in life. My rejection philosophy somewhat reminds me of that old, albeit childish, saying, "I'm rubber, you're glue. Whatever you say bounces off of me and sticks to you."

If someone says to you, "You don't pay enough attention to me" or "You don't buy me enough gifts", or flat out states, "You're not good enough for me", is that **purely** a reflection of you, the partner? Of course not. They are primarily a reflection of the speaker's needs. Most *everything* in life that people say are a reflection of their own needs. So, those above comments **also** mean, "I need more attention than you want to (or can) give," "I need more gifts than you want (or can) give," and "I need someone who can fulfill my needs."

The above speaker may indeed be *needy* with their desires, but no matter the exact situation, he or she definitely needs *more* of whatever "it" is. The "rejectee" simply either cannot or does not want to do those things for the partner here for whatever reason. The "rejector" can either change who they are and be less than fully happy, or find the right partner for them where the needs naturally meet on the same level. Or who knows? The rejectee may **want** to meet the needs of the partner without being constantly reminded, and may indeed put forth the effort on their own, without necessarily "changing" who they are and sacrificing too much. These are the three possible options. At any rate, Relationship Law #7 is: *Rejection is purely a reflection of someone's needs, no more, no less.*

Hopefully partners are somewhat tactful with one another when or if they do "reject" their partner in some way. Of course, that is not always the case. But whether it is intended or not, some sort of rejection will happen and many times **should** happen between couples. Any sort of grievance or complaint is a form of "rejection". A person is saying to another, "I need this from you, and I'm not getting it." And then they must work on it. It's when this complaint or grievance continues to be a problem that the couple should try to find help or perhaps just let the relationship go. Does that sound extreme? Maybe. But think about it. If you are a big conversationalist for example, and learn a lot through an exchange of ideas, is it really worth it to maintain a relationship with someone who can't do that with you? If you love being romantic and/or affectionate, and your partner is not that way, is it worth sticking around? If you love sex, and your partner not so much, is this a good match? There are hundreds of these types of conundrums to potentially deal with. What is the advantage of being in a relationship with someone if your relationship needs aren't being met? With or without your conscious awareness, if your needs are not met in your primary relationship, you *will* look for it elsewhere eventually, or be doomed to unhappiness within it, or both. So what's the point?

It's not horrible, cold-hearted, and negative to think that way. People are who they are. What's right for one partner might be wrong for the other partner. Everyone's needs are different. That's why, logically speaking, no one is truly rejected.

The only rejection happens to oneself, when an individual rejects *who they are as an individual entity* to remain in a relationship that is bad for them. This personal rejection can go the other way too. For instance, constant rejection of oneself may even put an end to a *good* relationship if one isn't careful.

The phrase, "It's not you, it's me," while cliché, is actually pretty true. But to be totally accurate, the phrase needs to be: "It's not you, it's *you and me together*." That is the actual situation. It doesn't sound great, but logically it's the truth. The similarities of two people's needs goes a long way in establishing a strong bond. Because without your needs fulfilled, you develop insecurities, which is a large obstacle to a strong bond. And this of course leads back to the aforementioned unhappiness and potential inattentiveness and even infidelity.

Once more, see how important taking care of your needs is?

To sum up this very important relationship gear, everyone has their relationship needs in addition to their individual needs. You may be wondering, "But Grant, you need to **compromise** in a relationship! Aren't you being a little harsh with your assessment of peoples' needs?" In a word, no. Maintaining a standard with your needs is extremely important. But as far as your "**wants**"…that's a whole other thing. But how do you discern between what you may want vs. what you may need in a relationship?

NEEDS VS. WANTS AND THE BIG THREE

When I go to college campuses around the country I always play a Dating Game to illustrate what is really important to the students when it comes to their dating lives. I have them identify a few of their needs, and then ask them to come up with three questions that pertain to those needs. Half the time, the contestants have a tough time coming up with really important questions for themselves. Rather, they settle for the obvious—"Where would you take me on a first date?"--the unimportant—"What kind of car do you drive?", or just the unnecessarily dirty, "How big are your breasts?"

Very little pertaining to their needs can be revealed by **any** answers to these questions.

Now, I understand that everyone's needs are different, but let me say for the record that the ***importance*** of the place one goes on a first date, the kind of car one drives, and the physical attributes one has is a lot less important than one thinks. Primarily because none of these things are permanent. If the contestant's looking for a ***short***-term dating scenario these may be needs at the moment, but if they are looking long-term, these are not truly needs for them. These qualities would be in the other category often confused with needs—"Wants".

A lot of people have a hard time identifying the difference between what they ***need*** and what they ***want*** in life. And in relationship scenarios, it becomes even more difficult.

Do you really *need* to go to a certain place on a first date?
Do you really *need* to occasionally ride around in a car of your choice? Do you really *need* for your partner to have certain physical measurements? At some point in your life, you may think so. But I'm willing to gamble that they're probably just *wants.* Again, everyone has different needs, but most likely those three above examples will never be "needed" by anybody. But even if you *do* think any of these qualities are necessary, with age and experience you will come to realize how unimportant some of those "needs" were.

The way to differentiate between your needs and your wants is to ask yourself: "Can I live *without* this thing in my life without harming my well-being on any level?" If the answer is yes, then this "thing" is a want. We all have **many** more wants than needs in life. However, if we cannot sacrifice something *without disrespecting and devaluing who we are as individuals,* than that certain something is indeed a need. If we can sacrifice something without cheating ourselves, then it's a want.

To simplify, *you can compromise things you want, you really cannot compromise things you need* (at least without paying for it later). Let this be called Relationship Law #8.

Some needs however are not realized until further analysis of an apparent superficial want is posed. A lot of times the contestants during my Dating Game ask questions that may seem pointless in some way, but upon deeper inspection, the question does indeed pertain to a need.

For instance, I've heard one female contestant say, "Tell me the funniest joke you know." A couple of people in the bachelor lineup couldn't think of any jokes, but one of them had a joke all set to go immediately. What the joke was isn't important (nor do I remember it), but the responses the contestants gave were. So what **is** the importance of making a joke on the spot like this?

One of the needs for the female contestant who asked this question was a sense of humor. That was an absolute necessity, because she has a huge spiritual need for laughter. However, the quick wit or memorized joke that was needed for that moment does not a funny man make necessarily. So, while the humor need is prevalent for her, the panelist who made the joke may not be that humorous of a person in most situations. He or she may seem too "practiced" in many situations as opposed to spontaneous and off-the-cuff. Plus, while many people may be funny in multiple ways, senses of humor may not match up well between two specific people. Put a person with a dry sense of humor together with someone who has a truly extreme and expressive sense of humor for instance. No matter how funny they may be individually, together they may not make a good match. At the same time, they may. Just like there are many attractive physical attributes, and a plethora of personalities, so are there many types of humor.

The point here is that the question that was asked could have been rephrased to provide a response that revealed a more thorough analysis of the "humor" need for that contestant. A better question may have been, "Who are your favorite comedians?" "What are your favorite comedies?" or to make it more personal and pertinent, "How would you treat me if I had a big drool spot on my face?" With these questions you may get more of an insight on how well your humor matches up with the other person.

Of course, asking a simple question during a dating game is no substitute for getting to truly know someone in a real-life situation. Most things worth anything take time. But that above example reminds me of one of the best questions I ever heard by a contestant. A girl asked her panel of men, "If we went out to eat at a nice restaurant, and we got dressed up really nice…and I had a huge zit on my back and I didn't realize it but you did, what would you do?" It is a specific situational question, yet there was a lot that was determined by the answers that were given. One of the guys said he'd ignore it, another said he would let her know it's there, and another guy said he'd make a joke about it. The guy making the joke about it would be taking the biggest risk in that situation, because not only was he bringing it to her attention, potentially embarrassing her, but he was making a joke regarding it as well, potentially humiliating her.

However, as it turned out, she placed honesty way above her personal comfort, and he made her laugh with the joke on top of that.

Guess who she chose.

Others would prefer in that situation to *not* know if they are "blemished" somehow. And of course, many would prefer the honesty, even in potentially embarrassing situations, **without** the jokes. But this particular girl found honesty, humor, and confidence very important in a man. Being able to diffuse a potentially embarrassing situation showed her a lot of character on his part. So this one question didn't tackle just one need, nor two, but at least a few needs for her. **That's** an effective question.

So, we've learned how to distinguish between needs and wants. We've also delved a bit into how being specific with conversation and interaction provides many more answers for you than if you asked general questions. Finally, we've learned how to identify what your needs truly are and how to identify which individuals can best fulfill those needs. And of course, this process always takes time and patience. Nothing can truly be answered by one well thought-out question. It's a process. Don't press, just take things one step at a time.

Now for the three needs that *everybody* needs. Other than having your individual needs fulfilled, there are needs which I call The Big Three. (Hopefully you've already identified them on your list of needs, but many people tend to overlook them) Those are: Love--kinda nice to have that in a relationship, eh? Healthy Communication--which I'll talk in depth about a few chapters from now. And the third, and arguably most important need-- Respect.

A lot of us don't think about that one.

I know I didn't for a long time.

I know that if I had to pick one need for a healthy long-term relationship that outweighs every other one, **Respect** would be it. Many of you I'm sure would choose Love, with Communication a close second.

This is my argument: Love is great and important, and very desirable, and I know I personally need that if I'm going to share my life with someone. But ultimately, you **can** have a healthy long-term relationship without it. It's not desirable, but possible. It's not possible to have a *healthy* long-term relationship without respect. Plus, as my ex-wife will attest to, love by itself is not quite enough. We had love in abundance. But I think we both didn't respect each other enough to keep things going, probably because we just couldn't understand each other and our needs enough, as much as we tried.

The most fulfilling relationships I've had are the ones where we've both had a ton of respect for each other. And, not coincidentally, they were the most honest and communicative relationships I've had as well. And that's why I believe Respect beats out Communication. If the Respect is there, the Communication (and honesty) will follow. And of course, if your needs pair up well with your partner, respect is much easier to attain.

So, Relationship Law #9 (and it's a biggie), is as follows:

HEALTHY COMMUNICATION

Comes out of….

RESPECT

Which is aided by…

UNDERSTANDING INTERPERSONAL NEEDS

Defined by…

PERSONAL NEEDS

Again, notice how everything good in a relationship stems from knowing your needs first and foremost? And also, notice how love is a separate entity from these things. This is why "being in love" cannot ever truly define how solid and long-lasting a relationship will be. That feeling, at its core, is an "energy high" and will most likely fade somewhat. The bond will not. Again, it's all about the bond.

FOURTH GEAR: BE WITH A BEST FRIEND

I know many of you read the above title and immediately had a strong reaction to it, one way or another. A good chunk of you probably either rolled your eyes, shook your head from side to side, or furrowed your eyebrows, or perhaps all of the above. And then there's a (hopefully big) group of you who nodded and said, "Preach on brother Grant!"

Well, maybe those weren't your **exact** words…

Those of you who are in an intimate relationship with a good friend need no further explanation here. It's those of you who vehemently disagree that need to be enlightened in this chapter.

When I say that the healthiest, longest-lasting relationships involve you and a best friend, you disbelievers probably automatically assume one of two things: 1) That you need to be best friends first with someone before dating them, or 2) You should give anyone who's a best friend of yours a try in the dating arena.

Uhh…no.

I believe that as long as two people *become best friends somewhere along the line of the relationship* then they have a good shot at making things work.

I don't care if the friendship is established months before the intimacy starts, days before it starts, or begins during the actual intimate relationship. It just needs to happen at some point. Everyone is different, so everyone's timing and particular path is different. Two of my most successful relationships in my life took two totally different paths. In one of them, the friendship developed during the relationship, and one relationship started months after the friendship developed. The timing didn't matter. What did matter was that the friendship indeed developed. And that's why those were the most "successful" in my eyes. Granted, they didn't pan out, but the friendship still was a huge benefit in each case. Not coincidentally, the break-ups were not horrendous, and we're still friends today. I've also learned the most in those relationships.

As for the second (and less-likely) misunderstanding of my point--just because two people hit it off in every way and are best friends, that doesn't mean you **need** to take things to the next level. As I stated in Chapter 2, don't "idealize" the relationship and make it more than it is. The foundation of a relationship is indeed there with a solid friendship, but the attraction, the love, and the relationship **needs** are still huge aspects to consider, and may not be elements that are present or work well in that particular situation. To illustrate the point again using the show Friends, just look at Rachel and Joey.

As close and intimate as these two are, their relationship needs are just too dissimilar (although arguably more alike than Rachel's and Ross', but I digress).

On the other end of the Friends' spectrum, Chandler and Monica had an extremely solid friendship for years prior to their relationship, and that is obviously the glue that held them together, even during troubled times. Both of those twosomes simply had different needs—one of the couples worked, and one of them didn't in accordance with their individual needs. So, closeness can, but does not necessarily, translate to an intimate dating relationship.

I think a lot of women and men confuse "closeness" and a solid bond with the need to be physically intimate. It is possible to be close with another person, and be attracted to them, but not necessarily make it a physical relationship as well. I have become *very* aware of those types of relationships over the years. Many of my friends, including my current girlfriend, is stupefied as to how I can have all these tight bonds with my female friends without having the relationships turn physical at any point. Ultimately, in most of those friendships, I would be ruining what we have by "making the relationship more than it is." Those relationships went as far as they should go—a deep friendship. That's what the bond dictated. The relationship needs, attraction, or love simply just wasn't strong enough to take any of those friendships to the next level. Sometimes bonds seem confusing, but again, the more time you take to identify it, the clearer it becomes.

The only other complaint I hear when I claim that people need to be with a best friend is: "But I want to keep the attraction and passion alive! I want my best friends to be friends, and my boyfriend/girlfriend to be more of a mystery.

It keeps the attraction fresh!" To that I must say two things: First off, I will always argue that the closer you are to someone, the more passionate and attractive that person becomes. So getting to know someone well definitely adds to the closeness. Secondly, if you still believe in the above quote, perhaps you aren't truly ready for the responsibility of a relationship. It's fine and sometimes necessary to have a little mystery, but a thorough knowledge of your partner needs to be at a **much** higher level than the "mysterious aspects" to truly keep things ticking and to keep the bond strong. Nothing lasts forever. And that includes physical beauty and mystery in a relationship. Sounds depressing, but looks do fade, and mystery becomes scarcer. This is especially why the bond and the friendship **have** to be there at all times. Once you identify your needs versus your wants in a relationship, you'll find that most, if not all, of them pertain in some way to friendship.

"What do mean exactly by friendship?"

To keep this very simple, think of all the qualities you value most about your best friends: honesty, good communication, comfort to be yourself, supportiveness, listening ability, talkativeness, humor, healthy conflict resolution, similar interests….you can name even more I'm sure.

Is there anything on that list, or that you can add to that list, that you don't want in a partner?

Probably not.

Just about all of those things fall back into the category of **respect** by the way. You respect your best friends, right? If you don't, then they're probably not **best** friends of yours…or they may not even be true friends at all to you.

So ask yourself simply, "Does my partner have those qualities I love most about my best friends?", and "Does my partner garner my utmost respect?" If not, you may want to address that somehow, and reevaluate the potential of your relationship.

THE BAG O' CRAP—ISSUES

Often during my live shows, I play a "Couples Game", which is much like the old "Newlywed Game" with a couple key differences. The first obvious one being that no one playing the game is married (not that it can't happen, but it's a rarity for me to see married couples at college together). Instead, I just use pre-married couples, whether they've been together 3 days or 3 years. The other key difference in my game is that I always use at least one "set" of best friends to compete against the couples. I usually ask three basic questions to one partner concerning the other, with the third question usually being the most interesting. That question is, "What is the one thing you two argue over, or disagree about, the most?" The interesting thing is, usually the couples have something they can easily point to, while the best friends have a hard time coming up with an answer. This is usually because either the best friends have such small petty disagreements that they are hard for them to remember, or the issues were not even worth bringing up. And the biggest reason friends have a tough time answering this question is because they usually don't disagree on **anything.**

Ahh…for such stress-free simplicity in a relationship of the intimate kind! How often do we forget or overlook problems from the past? Not enough probably. We often tend to hold on more than we should. And how often do we never disagree on anything with our lover? Never…if we are honest with ourselves and our partner anyway.

Best friends don't seem to have the same depth of problems as many couples do. (Yet another reason to formulate that strong friendship bond)

If there only was a way to keep things this simple with our *intimate* partners. Well, there is. Although it's going to be a wee bit more difficult to manage.

Why is that? Well, when an extra degree of emotions and energy are projected onto another, it's automatically going to make things more difficult. In other words, the depth of our emotional and energy bond with another causes this extra complication. Often times it is hard to keep the level of respect and communication going strong during times of stress with our partner. Since our emotions are closer to the surface with our partner, so are our vulnerabilities and our issues—or our bag o'crap.

I established back in Chapter 4 that we all have our issues. Our filters are rarely entirely clean. We are rarely going to see reality exactly the way it is. All we can do is try to keep it in clear and objective view as best we can as often as we can. But no matter how good our vision may be at any time, we still all have our blind spots.

Most of these blind spots are due to the fact that we may not be fulfilling some needs of ours at that particular time. Therefore, the pure "sunshine" of our happiness is being clouded. But there is one other reason that we all have our blind spots.

We are just born that way.

Depressing? Not necessarily. We **all** have strengths and weaknesses. For every strong point we have, there is a corresponding weak point. Or should I say a *potential* weak point. One of my stronger characteristics is that, for the most part, I am a pretty confident person. The potential weaknesses of this are that it is quite possible to become cocky, or possibly not be understanding of another's point of view, or perhaps to not be able to see and admit my wrongdoings. I am a good talker, so sometimes it's a struggle for me to shut up and listen. I also consider myself pretty logical. However, in the past it has been brought to my attention that I could, and should, be more open to my emotions.

I believe I have improved on these weak points of my personality over the years, but I know if I'm not careful, I could slip back into my bag o' crappy qualities! In fact, at times now I notice myself tipping too far in the *opposite* direction! So, keeping that balance is tough. Point is, for every strength, there is a potential weakness in all of us.

Every time we deal with any sort of a relationship, we have to remember that every person we encounter has their issues too. No matter how they come across, no matter what they share, no matter how "together" they may be, everyone has their bag. It's kind of another way of saying that we all "Put our pants on one leg at a time," or that we all "have to go to the bathroom at some point." Hence, there's no reason to truly feel intimidated by anyone, nor is there reason to ever "try" to intimidate anyone else.

We all have our fears and our crap to deal with.

Like I said at the beginning of this book, I am not perfect and never will be. And we're all in the same boat. It's okay, it's part of being human. But I know I will try my damnedest to keep my filter and bag clean.

As I alluded to in previous chapters, step one is for us to realize and acknowledge our issues. Step two is to somehow "accept" or gain a certain comfort with our insecurities. That isn't to say we should stagnate at this point though. So step three is finding a way to work through the issues-- having the desire to improve.

That's all we can ask.

Just know you'll never be perfect. Realize that (step one).

Find a way to be comfortable with that fact (step two).

And while the comfort may be attained, don't be satisfied. The satisfaction remains in the journey towards that ideal self you want. So don't lose sight of that goal. The third step—improving your imperfections—is the focus of the next few chapters.

MEN VS. WOMEN

"Men are assholes!" "Women are bitches!"—the most common descriptions provided when I ask what the difference is between the two genders.

Whether the people answering that question are joking, aren't putting much thought into it, or are just bitter, I hear that answer many times. Of course, I don't agree with this assessment at all. We all have the *potential* to act that particular way, but no, those words do not define our genders. Yes, we all do have that negative side, and interestingly enough, that negative side becomes illuminated most often and most clearly in an intimate relationship.

Again, every person in a relationship brings their baggage with them to it. So any interpersonal relationship between two people consists of *two* groups of issues that will have to be dealt with in some way. However, I maintain that when a *physically intimate* relationship occurs, a *third* group of issues is introduced into the situation.

How so?

Well, this group of issues comes about because of the aforementioned higher degree of closeness due to the energy and emotions involved, as discussed last chapter. Whether the relationship is a heterosexual or homosexual one, there are definite intimacy dynamics that arise.

In almost every relationship, there are more dominant and submissive energies, controlling and lenient personalities, powerful and relaxed spirits. I hesitate to use the terms "masculine" and "feminine" traits, because those stereotypes are for the most part, outdated and unfair. But there is no denying that the dynamics in **any** type of intimate relationships are fairly similar. Having said all of that, I will speak in the simplest way I can of the dynamic I am most familiar with—the heterosexual dynamic, since I am a heterosexual male. So for these next examples, I will define the *apparent* nature of men and women.

Hopefully these next bits of relationship knowledge do not come as a total surprise to you, but if so, then at least you'll be filled in.

Relationship Law #10 is as follows:

First off, **MEN ARE STUPID!**

We're just dumb. There's really no way around that. We need our hands held…a **lot**…figuratively speaking. We're a little slow on the uptake. You know what I mean ladies. Have you ever said anything to your man that took him hours, days, weeks, or even months to fully comprehend? Fill in your own answer, because there are too many to go into here. But you know what I mean. I remember my college girlfriend saying some piece of advice to me back in the mid-90's that I didn't understand until the turn of the century.

Yeah, as intelligent as I'd like to think I am, I'm still slow on some matters. But it's par for the course as far as men go though. It's not uncommon for males to be 5-10 years younger mentally (and emotionally) than they are physically.

But before all you guys get your panties in a bunch...

WOMEN ARE CRAZY!

Enough said.

Now that you **all** hate me...

Are things really this simple? Well, obviously not. I am, also obviously, generalizing. I'm sure you're asking, "Wait a second, isn't *this* stereotyping? Isn't this also outdated and unfair?" I don't think so, and I'll tell you why in a bit. But fret not! Not all of us are born this way. Just 99.9% of us. Not all of us remain this way all of our lives either. Just 99.8% of us. Okay, I'm exaggerating with these figures. But more often than not, we tend to all operate and act in accordance with our gender (or at least our "gender-energies"). We can work through this. But these are simply our natural states of being. Don't deny it. (Remember step one: acceptance)

Why *is* this our natural state? Well, two reasons: One is our environment. Family, friends, schools, and neighborhoods we're exposed to may have an influence on what roles you should play as a male or female. I would like to think that people are becoming a little more open-minded with their ideas of male and female roles in society. But the truth is this open-mindedness is not as prevalent as I would hope for as of yet.

The second reason for my "stereotypes" is a lot more pertinent and permanent (which is why I don't find this outdated): Biology. Our basic hormones are still the biggest reason for men's apparent "stupidity" and women's apparent "insanity".

For a quick recap of basic biology regarding men and women, here you go: men have testosterone. **Lots** of it. I don't know if you knew *this* fact though: Men, or shall I say male fetuses, have testosterone wrapping around their brains while in the womb. So, excuse the expression, but we men are screwed from the get-go! As a result, males are naturally "wired" for sex. You've probably heard the phrase that men are "hunters". Men are indeed more primal in many ways. I go as far as to say that men are like dogs. We look for attention wherever it is provided for us. If we don't get enough attention we either ask for more or go somewhere else to find it, and if we get too much attention we get bored and go away. And even if we're accustomed to a certain type of attention from someone, and then get bored and leave, we'll **come back** to that someone if we *stop* receiving that particular type of attention from them (remember that ladies…if you ever want your man to treat you well or pay more attention to you…the trick is to leave him be. He *will* come running back if he likes you. This method tends to work very well. Of course, the problem here is that you are playing games in that situation. Communication is of course a better and healthier method of receiving attention.)

At any rate, men are simpler creatures and tend to exist *in the moment* more than women generally do. So, our priorities and focus oftentimes are much different than what females tend to focus on. Lots of times it's sex first, everything else later. I figure that this "wiring" tends to *initially* keep men from focusing on anything deeper, like emotions for example. This is why men seem dumb to women. Sure, we may appear more logical and smart in other more superficial ways, but this lack of knowledge of dealing with women, emotions, effective communication, or ourselves, gives plenty of credence to my statement of "male stupidity".

On the flipside biologically, women produce much estrogen and are geared for reproduction, as opposed to just being geared for sex. Women are generally seen as more complex beings who are smarter, more tuned-in to their emotions, and occasionally tend to attempt to control and manipulate their environment a little more than men. So, the priorities tend to be different. Again, this isn't always the case, but more often than not it is. Usually, women are hormonally and subconsciously driven to explore themselves and their emotions to a much deeper degree than men. Of course, sometimes this promotes *over*-emoting. The menstrual cycle doesn't help with this either. Emotions aren't the easiest things to control, especially dealing with us men. Hence, ladies, you at least *seem* crazy to men (and sometimes to women as well).

The way I see it, it's like the chicken and the egg. Male stupidity leads to female craziness.

But also female craziness can lead to male stupidity …because you know, men tend to tuck tail and lose all sorts of strength during these times of crisis, making us look and feel quite stupid. How many times are men not prepared for an argument or disagreement, and are only able to spit out the words, "Uhh…I love you…" thinking that may fix the problem?

It's happened with me many a time, and I consider myself a *good* communicator! At any rate, men's stupidity is spurned on by female craziness too. And the cycle continues on and on. Women go crazier because we men don't understand something, which makes us feel even dumber, which makes them crazier…etc. Theoretically, the pattern can go on forever!

Another example I like to use to illustrate how we are geared is the example of a man and a woman out on a date. Let's say everything is ideal--the restaurant is fantastic, the movie is fun, emotional and thought-provoking, the conversation is unparalleled, and this all leads to a wonderful physical encounter of some type at the end of the evening. After they've parted ways, the next day the woman has typically already analyzed the date, has figured out how far the relationship can go, and if she sees potential marriage from this relationship, then she's already starting to plan the damn thing! As far as the man is concerned …well…after his morning scratching, he's basically just congratulating himself on a "job well done" while performing his own unique version of the "I Got Some!" dance. That's about as far as **he's** analyzed the night, and probably as far as he will analyze it for many dates to come.

Again, that's a generalization. But it is normally how we are geared. However, we can all evolve past these generalities.

Again, the first step to anything is acknowledging that an issue exists. So there it is, in front of your face for you to see. Now step two is up to you…to get comfortable with it.

I'll help you in the next chapter with the third step—taking steps to improve the situation.

THE FIFTH GEAR: COMMUNICATION
Talking Through Your Crazy and Listening Through Your Stupid

One of my **biggest** needs in a relationship is to be with someone who is able to work through their problems in a healthy and effective manner. Do I expect them to *not* have issues or bad days? Of course not. (Nor should any of you guys…remember last chapter?) But I *do* need a woman who can keep her issues in perspective, and a woman who can either work through them, with or without me.

That's where my quote, "talk through your crazy" comes from. You (my female partner) may be going nuts and might be freaking out right now, but do you have the presence of mind to work your way back down to reality somehow …with or without me? And if you complain, bitch, or actually talk about the problem(s) with me, can you let me help you? I've been with women who are able to talk through their problems with me, and been with those who could not, at least not with me. Guess which relationships I considered the best ones?

Granted, if your bond with your partner is strong, communication shouldn't normally be a problem. (Just make sure the bond isn't shaky due to your own insecurities.) But *everyone* has their moments when communicating with their partners isn't exactly easy. Even the best couples I know occasionally hit a communication stumbling block.

There are two simple and basic ways I like to deal with communication blocks.

The first is my version of the K.I.S.S. method. In other words, Keeping It Simple (for when you feel Stupid). And the "Stupid" is often appropriate here since this KISS method more often pertains to the male population than the female. It has been my experience that women seem to intuitively know what to say to help their partner out. Guys tend not to. (Again, we men are dumb.) The key to keeping things simple here, and not making them any worse, is to LISTEN. It took me about 30 years to learn that lesson! Sad but true. It's yet another reason men often look stupid to women.

Forgive me for possibly being a chapter late, but I believe that this particular Men vs. Women topic fits in better in this chapter: Men like to fix problems during conversation. Women just want you to listen. Thus, men need to "listen through their stupid." After all, believe it or not, listening tends to make people smarter.

However, I know men are men, and we naturally feel like we need to do **something** for any problem that arises. So this is going to take time for men to master, ladies. Unfortunate, but true.

Here's a typical way I used to deal with any issues in my relationships:

I would enter my girlfriend/wife's room and ask, "Hey sweetie, how's it going?" And often the response would be, "Eh..." or "Not good" or "I'm SO pissed off right now!" Of course, being the dutiful good boyfriend/husband I would ask, "What's wrong baby?" Then she would invariably say,

"Well, let's see...work sucks, school sucks, this place is a mess, my mom's pissing me off, my hair's a disaster..." etc. etc. (It could have been any or all of those things).

So I respond...

"Well, what if you lessened your work load by taking an extra day off a week? And I could help you with money if you really need it. Plus, that could free up some time so you can catch up with your homework! See! Two birds with one stone! And I'll help you clean this place up. And yeah...don't worry about your mom. She's having a rough day and will get over it. She's just worried about you 'cause she loves you, you know. And as far as your hair, just bathe more..."

Okay, I've never said that last part.

At least, I have not said it seriously in times of crisis.

But the point is I tried to help. Do you think I got a big, "Oh Grant, thank you so much! That really helps a lot! Thanks sweetie!"

Not so much.

Can you guess the response I normally received to my advice? Just picture a **loud** shrieky, shrill "voice" answering, **"GOD!! ARE YOU LISTENING TO ME?!? SHUT UP!!! CAN'T YOU JUST BE $@^&#% QUIET AND LISTEN?!?!?!?"**

At the time, I thought that's what I was doing. I just took it to the next logical step, and tried to help. It sounded good to me. Still does actually.

However, like I said, men and women are geared differently.

I found out years ago in therapy a way to remedy this sort of exchange. All it takes is one sentence: *"What do you need from me?"*

Of course, before you ask that question, **don't** interrupt your partner! Let your partner have their say. **Listen to all of it**. And then, when you are utterly confused and/or scared for your life, ask "What do you need from me?"

Your partner may look at you totally perplexed. However, this is not a bad thing. Often, your partner will be wondering what exactly it *is* they need from you. Also, your partner may say the words, "I don't know. I guess I just need to vent." This doesn't exactly answer the question as to what **you** should do, but in essence this translates to "Just shut up and listen".

Most of the time, women want you to **listen**. If you're in doubt, listen. But if you feel you should do more or are confused, ask the KISS question-- *"What do you need from me?"*

You may be surprised by your partner's answers. Sometimes, your partner may want your honest opinions. Sometimes, they'll actually want you to help fix the problem! But usually, your partner wants you to support them by listening, and will maybe even verbalize their need for a hug, cuddle, kiss, whatever.

But you'll never *know*…unless you ask the question. However, do **not** do anything *except* what your partner requests at that particular time. Just do what they ask and that's it! If you feel the need to continue the conversation for any reason (to resolve it for instance), do it later! The key is to help your partner relax and "find his/her feet" so to speak at that particular moment. The second key is to keep your connection healthy during this time. Fixing the the actual problem is actually a distant third goal, but that will come. And it will come a *lot* easier if the first two keys have been accomplished. (So, patience men!)

I have a personal issue with not being comfortable with uncertainty, or with situations that are in any sort of limbo. So the KISS communication method is something I still struggle with. Even *after* my divorce, I would still see my ex-wife and ask her again, "How are ya?" And she'd respond with something like, "Eh…my computer's acting up again." And my knee-jerk reaction of course would be, "Well, have you tried this…?" And she'd yell back, **"YES I'VE TRIED THAT!!"** Then I'd respond correctly with, "I mean…what do you need from me?" Of course at that point, she's pissed and I've missed my chance to help without making things worse first. (I find it extra ridiculous on my part that I would actually *try* to give advice regarding computers, since she's the computer wiz and I'm barely beyond toddler level with them!)

The other wonderful effect of asking this particular question is that it shows your partner that you *are* listening, *do* care, and *do* want to help. Plus, now the ball is in your partner's court.

Your job for the moment is done. So the responsibility is now up to the "complainer" to answer their partner with what it is they need to the best of their ability. And "What do you **think** I need?" is not an appropriate answer by the way. People…men especially…are not mind readers! At this point guys, you are well within your rights to respond with, "I would have appreciated an answer to my question, but since you have none forthcoming, I will leave you alone until you let me know how I can help you." Or at least something to that effect. Then simply give your partner space.

I assure you, when they're ready to chat, they'll find you.

So there is responsibility by both parties here. Listening must transpire, as well as "the KISS question", and a genuine effort must be made in response by the initiator of the complaints. The key again, is maintaining the connection between the couple during this troubled moment in time. This prevents things from getting worse later on. No bitterness or resentment builds. But if you and your partner are facing a particularly difficult issue, or just need a stricter structure for communicating effectively during troubled times, I have an even better method…

The Mirroring Technique

This concept may be nothing new to many of you who have either been through some sort of counseling and therapy, or to those of you who actually *are* counselors and therapists.

I learned it while in marriage counseling years ago, and I must say that even though my marriage didn't work out, this mirroring process accomplished two very important things:

First, we remembered why we loved each other so much. This made our last year or so probably the best we've ever had together. And secondly, and quite ironically, it helped us realize ultimately that we ***weren't*** meant for each other, which in turn led to our much needed separation.

How did mirroring do this so successfully? Because the technique helps you look at yourself and your relationship honestly, by getting to the heart of the matter more quickly than you normally would otherwise. Mirroring doesn't allow for the factors that cause communication breakdowns to take effect.

Again, after a lack of personal happiness, the next biggest reason relationships falter is due to communication breakdown. The three biggest signs of communication breakdowns are as follows: Arguments tend to escalate, Sarcasm is used inappropriately, and Issues are not being addressed. Mirroring prevents all three from occurring, assuming that the couple sticks to the mirroring rules.

Ideally both people are relatively calm prior to mirroring. However, this technique by its very nature does help the partners to calm down anyway, so being calm prior to mirroring is not imperative. And this is the simple procedure:

- Both people face each other within close proximity. (Preferably within arms reach)
- The person who needs to introduce the issue (the speaker) speaks. Just one, two or three sentences maximum.
- The listener repeats what the speaker just said back to them. It doesn't have to be verbatim, but the thoughts need to be returned as accurately as possible back to the speaker. The listener asks, "Is that right?" The speaker responds "Yes or No".
- If the answer was "No", the speaker needs to repeat what they said again. This process is repeated until the listener responds sufficiently enough for the speaker to honestly respond "Yes" to the question "Is that right?"
- Once the listener repeats the information accurately and gets "Yes" as an answer from the speaker, the listener then asks, "Is there more?"
- The speaker either answers "Yes" and continues with the next point or answers "No" and then switches roles with the listener so the listener's side is heard. The process is then repeated with the listener as the new speaker and the speaker as the new listener.
- The mirroring process can end at the discretion of the partners at any time they choose.

That's basically it.

It seems simple, and in a way, it is. But that's the point. Communication is best when it's simple and unruffled by tangents and unimportant facts, unhindered by anger and by people not listening.

However, this technique may also seem boring to some of you. But I'll tell you, it's not at all. If it **is** boring to you, there's probably no need for you to mirror in the first place, primarily because it's not a potentially emotional situation.

Even if this initially sounds boring to you, do you at least see how this process helps out the speaker and listener? The speakers can feel free to express whatever feelings, thoughts, or observations they want at whatever pace they want without fear of interruption or criticism. Also, when the listener repeats the information back to them, it helps the speaker realize how something sounds. Sometimes, the speaker will say, "Huh…that sounded stupid." Or they'll take back something they said, or state something in another way. So, the "listening" portion of the "speaking" is quite valuable here too. Likewise, the person temporarily in the role of listener is truly forced to **listen** and thereby not formulate a counter-argument. And the speaker will know when the listener is formulating that counter- argument, because the listener won't be able to repeat what the speaker says. Remember, you can't effectively state your side as a listener until you successfully *listen* in the first place. Such are the rules and advantages of the mirroring technique.

Often when I demonstrate mirroring to someone I choose one person from the crowd to relay a problem. I take the role of listener first. A common mistake made by most speakers I deal with comes in the form of babbling about the issue and not keeping it succinct. You *can* ramble, but you have to do it in **small increments** while mirroring.

Not only so your partner can understand what you're saying, but so *you* can understand what you're saying. It's easy to get lost on tangents or miss the point of what you're trying to say when you babble. So obviously, your partner may be lost as well.

Other times speakers have no idea what to say. In which case, I'll tell them to just tell me the problem. And that's all they do…at first. And that's fine. Many of them tend to elaborate the longer the mirroring lasts, although it's not imperative to do so. You don't have to say a lot, all you need to do is say *something.* After all, you are mirroring for a reason. So introducing the reason works just fine to get the conversational ball rolling.

Of course, the most entertaining moments during my demonstrations are due to the listeners. The audience laughs most often at this…not to make fun of the listener, but because the "listening guffaws" strike all too close to home for them. They see with their eyes and ears how ridiculously obvious it is that a lack of effective listening becomes an impediment to effective communication. We all have made errors while listening. Sometimes while I am speaking on stage I am interrupted by the listener, which is a no-no. More often I'm given the counter-argument in response immediately after I'm done speaking. Another no-no. And **most** often I'm presented with someone who gives me *their interpretation* of what I said. Again…no. **Just repeat!** Mirroring is not the way we're taught to listen and communicate while growing up, so it seems unproductive.

However, it *should* be the way we're taught, because it's actually extremely productive! It *promotes* listening and only then can truly effective communication ensue.

Again, I'm not saying you need to conduct all or any of your conversations you have with others in this way…that is, if you already know how to listen. But **way** too many of us don't know how, especially during times of stress. So, we should get into a habit of at least repeating words to ourselves, if not out loud, to make sure we have listened. My mom did this with me when I was a toddler. It kept things simple, and if I had a point to make at that age, she would have eventually understood it. And as far as I was concerned, even if I made no sense at the time, I still knew my mom was listening, and hence cared for me. To this day we have a great connection, and we *still* unconsciously mirror with each other. (Of course, that may be more due to the fact that we're going deaf in our advanced ages, but I digress…)

Point being, we as a race are not trained to listen to others. And many of us don't even listen to ourselves! (And I'm convinced the world would be so much better off if we knew how to listen, but that's for another book) Of course, you first need to be comfortable with yourself, and honest with yourself to make this an easier process. Hence, my opening chapters of the book.

Before I continue, I want to relay my favorite example of mirroring I have ever witnessed and the effect it had on communication.

I was in Pennsylvania doing a show a while back and I needed volunteers to show the mirroring technique to everyone. I normally demonstrate the technique near the end of the show, so at this particular one I had already been talking for 50 minutes or so. And during that whole time, I had noticed a tension-filled couple in the back row. They were obviously a couple, so I invited them up. Once I brought them up, I explained the concept of mirroring to them, and asked the guy to bring up "an issue" he wanted to talk about. I was very careful about not saying things like, "I've noticed you two aren't happy campers right now," or "What is it that's troubling you?" Even though I knew they weren't happy and had a **large** point of contention to discuss, I didn't want them to feel any pressure whatsoever to discuss the situation in front of a crowd of people.

Somehow though, I figured they would discuss the problem anyway. And they did.

The guy proceeded to talk about his jealousy issue he had with his girlfriend. And when I say "talk", I mean he said two sentences. By that time, he started tearing up. And then his girlfriend started tearing up. When she repeated the words back to him, the waterworks broke loose…for both of them. And the audience was in the same boat, their sympathies very obvious to us on stage. After she accurately repeated these words her boyfriend said, she took her turn to speak. She said one thing, which her boyfriend repeated, and you could just feel the connection between the two reestablish itself. The fear and tension had been replaced by love and an ease of being.

The walls had come down. I asked the crowd, "You see how this can work?" Everyone nodded. It doesn't necessarily take much time to reconnect and communicate effectively with this technique.

After the show, I noticed a distinctly different vibe between the two people, and told them to continue mirroring if they needed to come up with a solution to their dilemma. They thanked me and left the room hand-in-hand, rejuvenated and optimistic. To be honest, I don't know if they are still together today, but I know that wherever they are today they are more comfortable with their situation than they would have been otherwise. And they now have the tools to handle any future communication complication that arises.

The beauty of this technique is that even if you aren't an effective communicator, or even if you aren't comfortable or honest with yourself or your situation, this technique will help with all of that. And even more importantly, it can reestablish the "connection" between partners. It's a very powerful tool to use.

EASY AND EFFECTIVE COMMUNICATION
Stems from…
PERSONAL HAPPINESS (COMFORT WITH SELF)

Stems from...

HONESTY WITH SELF

All of the above happens during mirroring.
I'm sure that you may still have some questions regarding the mirroring technique. Hopefully, I'll anticipate some of them here~

First of all, do **not** introduce the technique **while** you are in the midst of an argument. I've learned from first-hand experience that this does not work. Instead, introduce the technique when there are no immediate points of tension between you and your partner. If possible, you may want a third party there whom you trust the first time or two you attempt it with your partner. And obviously, they should know the rules as well. They can, in a way, "referee" the situation if some rules aren't being followed.

Speaking of not following rules, if one or both partners have a hard time speaking and listening in accordance with the mirroring structure, that may "turn up the heat" in the conversation. The whole point of mirroring is to *avoid* arguments and distractive emotions. So if anger erupts, it's best to take a break and agree not to speak until you can successfully mirror again.

Another thing I personally like to do is to continue this technique beyond the "airing grievances" stage, and use it through the "problem-solving" stage, like I suggested to the couple from Pennsylvania. Yes, this technique also works for finding compromises to problems.

But you can end the process whenever you prefer. You *can* end mirroring when you both get your points across. But you might try to also "problem-solve" in this fashion as well. Mirror until you find a solution that works for both people. This may take some time, but it will take a **lot less** time than it would take otherwise trying to work out a solution. And my whole philosophy is, why waste time? If you have a problem, solve it. (I know, I know, it's my guy-side coming out.)

Finally, let me reiterate that no, you don't have to mirror every time an issue comes up. Ideally, two partners can communicate without needing to "mirror" and just talk instead. Eventually this communication should develop naturally. But if you need to mirror, **DO IT**! Remember, even when you are "just talking" to solve a problem, you are still using these fundamental rules of communication—keeping talking simple, staying open to your partner, listening to your partner, and ultimately getting on the same page. That's the point of mirroring, keeping the connection between you and your partner by getting on the same page. You may not necessarily agree with what's on the page, and may not even understand your partner's language, but at least you're on the page.

My ex-wife and I spoke different languages apparently, and also disagreed a lot on issues. But mirroring was the best thing that ever could have happened to us. Disagreements became tolerable, and almost enjoyable. We would more easily see each other's point of view, and developed an understanding that wasn't there in the prior years together.

In the first ten minutes of our first mirroring session with our counselor, I remembered why I fell in love with her after a year or so of being out of love with her. It brought us back to our "happy place" while at the same time helping us see why we wouldn't work out for the long term. So, instead of breaking up and maintaining a bitter relationship to this day (or worse, *staying* together in a bitter relationship), we have ended on a relatively happy note and are still good friends today.

I have one more point to make regarding one of the "listener" issues I brought up earlier: How many times have you started a counter-argument with somebody and not heard what the other person said? I have…many many times. Often we are so concerned with getting our point across to the other person that we think about what *we* need to say while we should be listening to what the other person's saying.

Communicating is not about who's right or who's more valid or who has the better argument. It's about both people being **heard** and feeling **respected** in that situation. Right and wrong and all of that will take care of itself later. We're not always right, we're not always wrong. Almost 100% of the time, no one is 100% right or wrong in any disagreement. (Unless of course you're discussing math problems or something of that nature) Ultimately you have to ask yourself what is more important: you being right, or maintaining the connection with your partner?

Unfortunately, taken away by the heat of the moment, we often pick the former. But it's **much** better for your relationship to try and understand the other person's point of view. And that is done with a lot of listening. "Listen through your stupid" indeed!

Relationship Law #11: Talking through your issues is ALWAYS better than holding things in…always.

SELF-CHECK Q&A— COMMON QUESTIONS

There are obviously a ton of nuances about relationships that I haven't delved into thus far in this book. And there will be other subtopics that will still not have been explored when you finish this reading. However, I will do my best to cover some huge relationship points that I am often asked about in this chapter. Everything from dating, to sex, to marriage, to splitting up, and the underlying processes motivating our relationships.

Here we go:

1) How do you suggest going about the dating process?

A loaded question to be sure. But the answer would be for every person to date "according to their gifts" really. Find someone to date in the most natural way possible--**JUST DO THINGS YOU NATURALLY DO BECAUSE *YOU* WANT TO DO THEM, AND DO THINGS YOU HAVE NO PROBLEM DOING ON YOUR OWN.** If you go places out of doors that aren't natural for you, chances of you actually "picking up" a guy or girl probably aren't very good. For instance, if bars aren't your thing, don't go to them. Of course you can try new things, and you may enjoy the bar scene more than you thought you would, but if you *know* you don't really enjoy something, it *will* be noticeable to others, and that's a major turn-off for them.

Also, if you go someplace with the *intent* of finding someone there to potentially date, you might be similarly disappointed. Some people are able to do that for a variety of reasons (and more power to them), but that won't work consistently for most people. Again, if you do what comes naturally for you, the energy will flow the way it's supposed to, and **that's** when things tend to happen.

Independence is the key. Do what works for *you*, and do what feels *natural* for you. Personally, I love dancing, hanging with friends, exercising, and watching sports. I've met very special people in my life doing all of these things. And of course, there's always school, the workplace, and everyday situations like grocery shopping or just running into somebody on the street that may occur as well. So there **are** opportunities, you just have to keep your eyes and spirit open, without being *desperate* for that chance encounter. Remember, desperation and neediness are not very attractive traits.

As far as what to do on a date when you go out on one…again, that's up to your style. If you enjoy the romantic ones, do them. If you enjoy the casual-chill sort of situations, do those. Again, your date **will** be able to tell if something doesn't come naturally to you. That may be endearing on the one hand, but there's nothing more appealing than showing who *you are* in *your element*. Show your strengths from the beginning, but don't be egotistical about them. And by strengths, I don't mean how *physically* strong you are, or how good you may be at eating the food or driving the car. Don't be obnoxious or "showy". Rather, your strengths of *personality* should be revealed—your sense of humor, your selflessness, your confidence, or simply your smile can do wonders.

As far as your weaknesses, just be honest about them if they come up either in your conversation or your activities. Your date probably will appreciate the honesty, just don't harp on your negative attributes too much. The "poor me" routine doesn't work so well. To sum up, the more strengths you have that you can **show** your date, the better, but don't lie about your weaknesses or pretend you don't have any.

Some people are "daters" and some are "relation shippers." If you are part of the latter group, don't make the actual act of *dating* a priority. What I mean is, **take your time** and try not to date more than one person at once. Know who you are and don't overextend yourself. Also, do not smother the person you're dating or allow yourself to be smothered. Most of us have done some smothering in the past I'm sure. And you know who you are…the ones who call the second you get someone's phone number, or call multiple times a day if you can't reach someone (emergencies excepted of course), or the person who gets so excited if someone kisses you that you obsess over the next time you will see that person again. Basically, anyone who tries to make any step in the dating process **much** bigger than it is…that's a potentially smothering situation. You have to relax and not push.

The biggest thing with **any** stage of dating and relationships is to take things one step at a time. I know some people who confuse a kiss or a phone call with being in a relationship.

Wherever you are in a dating situation is where you are, no more and no less. While it may be fun to fantasize about the future possibilities, you still have to live in the present.

Talented baseball teams can talk about what being in the World Series may be like, and may enjoy the thought of it, but they need to focus on the next game, for if they don't, they may never make it to the big games. Take care of the present, or the future ideal may never happen. One game …er…date…at a time. So, while a kiss may mean so much more than just a kiss to you, you **have** to realize it's still ultimately just a kiss. You can't know where things will go until they get there. You can have strong feelings regarding future events, but facts are facts. What **is** is all that matters and all you can really work off of.

Okay…I've beat another horse beyond dead I think…

How do you *know* then if someone is *truly* into you? I'll explain it a little further with my next point, but ultimately when another person puts in the *effort* and *time* of his/her own accord to get to *know* the deeper you, you will then know if they are into you. If you have to ask for it or push or trick them into it, you're not getting a good read on them. If your date is continuously self-motivated to be with you, talk with you, learn about you, then they are probably into you.

Notice how I mentioned nothing about their desire to be with you physically. Honestly, physical desire doesn't translate into relationship potential. And if the physical is the first priority on the other's agenda, you may want to rethink your relationship plans with that person.

If you can hold off on getting close physically for a few weeks or so—maintaining a certain physical distance—you will **definitely** know what kind of person you are dating by the end of that time.

I couldn't begin to count how many dating situations didn't blossom because of the lack of patience one of the people (usually the guy) had with the physical aspect. I have a friend who used that sexual impatience as the main criteria for whether she dated someone long-term or not. Good for her…and now she's one of the few friends I have who's happily married. So, that's an easy way to see if someone is serious about you.

Like I've said before, many people equate physical love (eros) with true unconditional love (agape) or confuse it with just a basic functional relationship. Even many of you reading these words have done this or are in the process of doing that right now. You may be agreeing with me in principle, but quite a few of you may be subconsciously doing the same thing in reality. You may be hoping the physical leads to something else down the road, or banking on the physical bond to keep you going. I have had friends stuck in that mode for years, hoping for the "eros" to turn into something bigger and better (the "agape"), but it never happened. And I know I have done that subconsciously in the past too.

Why does that attitude exist for so many couples? One of the reasons is because the physical aspect is often one of the most **fun** aspects of a relationship, and people normally don't want to give that up.

But essentially, physical interaction is an *energy exchange,* and it is the *easiest* way to exchange and build energy. And with energy comes what? Attention and happiness--the main ingredients I talked about for a solid relationship.

However, there is more to a relationship than the sex. A healthy sex life **is not** and **cannot** carry a relationship. Unfortunately, some relationships don't have any other healthy workable elements to them, so sex is the only element both partners can rely on for fun and relaxation. Hence, the physical relations can be habit forming (more on that later).

In addition to being a "fallback" position in unhealthy relationships, sex can be addictive because the feeling derived from it can become emotional. Now hopefully there is some semblance of emotion leading *into* sex so the two categories are not confused, but if there is very little emotion leading into an encounter, the result can be emotionally confusing. *Sex promotes a high energy level that is often equated with another high-energy mode...which is love.* I'm not going to tell you what love is or even try to describe it. Love is something which we all learn about in our own ways throughout life, and there are many different types of love as well, which we all interpret in our own ways, according to our filters. But I **will** maintain that it too involves a high-energy exchange and building process. Therefore, it's easy to become confused on a subconscious level.

Physical intimacy may bring true closeness and emotions along with it, yet it may not. However, physical intimacy **always** brings an energy exchange. And remember, good energy does not equal love. So be careful of that misinterpretation. Again, take your time.

I believe you can't go too slowly in a relationship, only too fast. (And I don't mean to upset all of you in a happy marriage who married young or married quickly, or both. More power to ya! But you are a rare breed.) Relationships just take time to bloom, and it's normally safer to be patient. Every couple is indeed different, and things can work if you move fast, but I would never be the one to advise that route.

At any rate, my point with all of these dating tips is to know who you are and to be that person to the fullest before, during, and after your dates. Know your needs and you'll figure it out if the person you are dating is a keeper or not. (Gears #2 & 3)

2) What are the biggest warning signs that you are dating the wrong person?

Well, first off…there are **soooooo** many. I already mentioned a big one—if their time, energy, and focus is not on the *deeper* you (meaning that their focus on the "physical" you is not to be counted as someone who is serious about you).

I divide warning signs into two categories: the yellow flags, and the red flags. The red flags are more obvious…when your partner deeply disrespects and invalidates you and your needs--this is a rather nice way of saying it.

To put it bluntly, if your partner is hateful, uncaring, and/or abusive, that is being extremely disrespectful. And by abuse I mean physically, mentally, spiritually, or emotionally.

If you are being insulted, degraded, and criticized often, or if you are abused at all, either confront your partner to work it out, get help, or leave your partner **immediately**.

Less obvious are the yellow flags—not immediately obvious, but something to be wary of. It's possible to be disrespected in much subtler, non-abusive ways. For instance--an unthoughtful comment, a lack of listening, or even carefree teasing can unintentionally be disrespectful. And I've already discussed the importance of communication and personal happiness. If your partner has problems with either of these areas, they could lead to the red flags in the future. If you cannot find that "best friend" respect and acceptance from your partner after a couple years of dating, it's probably not going to be ideal for the long haul.

Now for the commonly overlooked things: I personally don't trust people I meet who compliment me a lot right at the outset of meeting me. Nor do I trust them if they give me gifts early on in the dating process. I call this "buying a relationship". I don't trust being on either end of this process. This applies to people my friends meet and date as well. I can't recall a single person of this "overly generous" mold who worked out with me or a friend of mine. And many situations didn't make it past a first date. I personally believe someone who gives compliments and gifts freely is either covering up for some other inadequacy or relationship deficiency, "or ironically doesn't really care for the other person at all (simply because it sounds like a possible secret agenda is present.) "

I know this sounds paranoid, but I'd rather trust someone who is *real at all times.* If someone is **too** into you, it's commonly a sign of not loving themselves enough, or of "loving" themselves **too** much (meaning that in reality they're very selfish and egotistical).

On the even less obvious side of things (but still related) beware of sentence-repeaters. These aren't necessarily even yellow flags…but they're something to be aware of. If anyone says anything more than twice within a short span of time, there is probably an underlying issue somewhere there. For instance, if someone says, "I haven't gotten 'any' in a long while" a few times, that's a sign that they **really** miss it, and you could be the next target (which may be fine with you, but on the other hand it may not be). If someone says, "I'm too nice for most people," over and over, they are obviously fishing for a compliment. If someone says, "I'm fat" a few times, there is an insecurity there. Even innocuous comments repeated over and over can reveal a lot about a person.

If someone asks, "Do you think I'm pretty?" a lot, obviously there is a self-confidence issue here that alerts you to that person's self-image. If someone says, "I like shoes," then…uhh…they just like shoes a lot. But they also may be hinting that they want **you** to buy them some shoes. Sometimes a spade is just a spade, but there's always a motive for it.

For some reason, that person is intent on making you notice that thing they're talking about. That's not a big deal, but anyone who repeats any statement more than twice has a definite reason for it, and many times they aren't even conscious of it.

And of course, chronic complimenters fit in this category as well. Be aware of all of these and what these repeated statements can mean. Just take note of things you've heard before, and ask yourself, or even the other person, "Why are you saying this?"

The same yellow flags should apply to any body language of another person too. We are drawn much more to body language and bodily energies than we think we are, and respond more instinctively to these signs than the verbal ones. However, just like verbal clues that we don't pick up on, we can overlook the motivations with body language and energy as well. If there is a lot of physical contact—a touch, a squeeze, a willingness to hug, or kiss—there probably is an interest there. Especially if you notice a distinct difference between how that person treats others relative to you. For instance, a hug for you from another person may seem like nothing until you find out that that person rarely hugs anyone else ever.

This physical attention may all sound great, but especially on "first contact" with another, you have to question the motivations involved, especially if you're a woman. Again, men are geared differently, and testosterone is a brutal thing to contend with! Seriously.

If a man is touching you a lot without much talking, you should know what you're getting into, for good or ill. (Of course, you may like that…) But the point is: do not ignore all the signs someone presents to you. It's easy to assume or wish for pure, altruistic motives and results based on what people do or say. But the reality is people are not perfect, and they compensate for their weaknesses and insecurities in many ways.

And most depend on the energy and attention from others to get that. Like I said in Chapter Six, this can become a drug. **You** can become the drug. Sounds great perhaps, until you realize you have little energy left for yourself and have been dragged down with your partner. But we've covered this. I just wanted to remind you of the dangers of not performing checkups on yourself and your relationship periodically.

I'm not saying you should go through all relationships or potential relationships paranoid. But these are just signs to take note of until you see the reality underneath the person, and that's going to take time. I know that I have a tough time maintaining patience in a relationship. I like to gather as much information as I can as quickly as I can.

Again, I don't like to waste time, and I also have an anxiety issue with regards to "living in limbo" that I'm trying to work on. But I do understand that I cannot expect quick answers and I understand that I will not receive full disclosure on someone until a lot of time has passed. Ultimately, I think reality-checks at every stage of a relationship are necessary to maintain perspective on your life and how you're doing.

3) Besides personal happiness, a strong bond, and solid communication, what other qualities bode WELL for a relationship?

I know I've focused a lot on warning signs and how to address issues. But there are positive things about relationships as well! Yeah!! **Really!!!**

Seriously, something that I also believe is very important for both partners is to get along with their partner's friends and family. The importance of this has grown more and more every year for me. Not only does it make things easier for everyone involved, but relating to all of them well is a sign that you and your partner can definitely have a bright future. Any issues you have with your partner's friends or in-laws are a potential sign of issues you may have with your partner at some point. *Especially* in regards to family. Any unhealthy dynamic your partner has with their parents, or that your partner's parents have with each other, may quite easily be passed down to your relationship. That dynamic which is learned early in life is hard to break later on.

The largest factor remaining for a healthy relationship consists of how much you and your partner stay "off the leash". This goes back to Relationship Law #3: ***The less you and your partner try to control each other, the better.*** This also goes back to respecting your partner, which in turn leads to trust, and finally leads to that freedom that so many couples aspire to, but so few truly attain. And I don't mean the freedom to go and sleep with whoever they want, that's not what I'm talking about.

Rather, the *freedom to be who they are*. Of course, if part of who your partner is consists of being an unfaithful sexual deviant, then it's better to find that out sooner than later, right? So you better take the leash off anyway.

That's what I don't understand about many couples. Obviously if you're insecure about your partner, then there is a problem. Try to talk about it, try to analyze it, and try to fix it, by yourselves or with outside help.

And if you can't fix it, take a break. But **don't** rein in your partner and stop them from being who they are. Many people think that this could be "saving the relationship", but in truth, it's really harming the relationship and the two people involved. Usually unbeknownst to the couple, every time a freedom to pursue "one's" needs is restricted, resentment develops. Every time one is "reined in" by their partner, resentment builds. Each time it builds, so does an additional wall between the two people, cutting off the level of love and respect and trust the two have left for each other. Everyone has a breaking point somewhere.

My advice: If you feel the need to "make" your partner do something, don't. If it happens to be a need of yours, talk it over, and try to fix it.

If you can't fix it, take a break. If it's just a "want" of yours, find a way to let it go. But if you are trying to mold your partner in your own image…sorry, but you're disrespecting that person. *People are not possessions*, no matter what the "label" (ie. *My* wife, *my* boyfriend, etc. Another reason I don't like labels).

I understand that there is a difference between trying to help someone evolve for *their* own good and trying to make someone change for *your* own good. But it's a very fine line at times. You can't have selfish motives. I know love is tough to explain and define, but I **do** know that true love isn't selfish. Even when you're trying to genuinely help someone, you have to be careful to not be pushy. Everyone evolves at different rates in different ways. The best way to lead, as always, is by example. So, no matter what your intentions and motivations with another, you need to be careful.

By the way, a lot of us say we trust our partners, but we really don't. Most of us are a little insecure and **don't** fully trust certain situations in our relationships. But I would say that the distrust is not primarily focused on our partners, but rather on our reaction to a situation. Meaning, *it's not that we don't trust our partner, rather we don't trust our reactions to what our partner may or may not do.* We don't think we would handle many situations well that our partner may or may not bring about.

To this I still say, "Do not punish your partner for this, and just let him or her be." It's not your partner's fault that you are insecure. And likewise, it's not your fault if your partner is insecure. If you are truly secure, you will be fine with most situations that most others may get jealous over, or you will recognize that you truly *can't* trust your partner, realize you deserve better, and let that person be on their own…and break up the relationship.

That's all easier said than done, of course. But that is the fact of the matter as I see it.

But back to trying to *change* someone--Wouldn't it be a lot simpler to find someone who fits the mold in the first place? Wouldn't it be more enjoyable not to battle over your needs constantly? It would probably be a lot less taxing to find someone who naturally wants to do what you want to do, wouldn't it? If you truly care for the other person and respect them, you owe it to them to be as fair and courteous as possible. So instead of nagging, or telling them what they should be doing, let them be.

You got with this person because you loved them just the way they are? Right? If you didn't, you're in the wrong situation. If you did...

...then **DON'T CHANGE THEM**.

Don't worry...I've done the same thing...as most of you have done or will do later on. I have been selfish, and had not realized it. Being in love can confuse you. And honestly, the fact that you don't know what's out there for you as far as a potential partner is concerned also contributes to "losing yourself" and having "control dramas" like those mentioned above. It's hard to believe the exact person for you is out there when you haven't met them, so we tend to make the best of who we have with us, even if they're not right for us. It's **very** easy to do. True and healthy love between two people is much more than just an emotion, it's also a way of *being.* Ultimately it truly has to *make sense* if it's to flourish and reach its potential. It doesn't make sense if leashes are being placed on the partners.

4) You've mentioned "taking a break" fairly cavalierly over the course of the book. Why?

Everyone tends to think of taking time off from a partner as such a horrible thing. It really isn't. It hurts sure. But it can do **way** more good than harm in a relationship. People assume that once you're "on a break" that it's over. A lot of times it is. But I'm sure you know others who get back together after breaking up all the time. Maybe you have in your own life too.

While I do believe in the "three strikes/break ups and you're out" policy (or "two strikes" for me personally), I also believe that *taking a break* can be the most useful thing one can do for oneself and even the relationship.

Notice I did not say break **up**. "Breaking up" is *intended* as a more or less *permanent* break. But whether it's taking a break in the midst of a relationship, or actually breaking up, taking time away is of the utmost importance in many cases. Each individual needs to "bring the energy" back to themselves. Everyone needs to re-center their attention. You have to learn how to pay full attention to yourself again. Clear your head in other words. And so does your partner, ex- or otherwise. You can reevaluate yourself and your needs without distraction much better when no one is around to influence you.

I would advise that if you go through many problems and are considering actually breaking up with your partner, attempt simply taking a break instead.

After talking through things during a crisis period, don't necessarily break up... take a break. Definitely take a week away. For more serious issues, I would say take about a month. That's enough time normally to sort things out. I **guarantee** you that you'll feel differently and see things more clearly after a month. Whether the "differently" part is better or worse, who's to say...but it will be different. For those of you following my Friends analogies, I'm sure "taking a break" may strike a negative chord for many of you. After all, Ross cheated on Rachel when she suggested a break.

But those two were way too immature to be together at that point in their lives, as his "relations" with another woman illuminated his insecurities and instability that would have just made a continued relationship between the two ungodly stressful at best. Just look at their attempted reconciliation later on that year--a disaster.

Again, you find out a **lot** about a person if you give them their freedom. You see what they are made of, and if it's not much, then it's better to find that out sooner rather than later. That doesn't mean that later on there won't be growth by the other person, but why suffer through a situation like that when they can grow more quickly and thoroughly as a person on their own? Trust me, if the connection and love is truly meant to be, you **will** be reunited in time. Don't disrespect yourself in the process, while hampering your individual growth and your partner's.

At any rate, it's too easy to become distracted and fall back into the same old patterns if you are constantly around your partner.

In essence, it's **very** tough to grow this way. It takes a lot longer to happen. So, if you fail to resolve your issues after continually trying to talk through the problems, it's very important and necessary to actually physically separate and **not** talk anymore for a while.

For example, in the aftermath of my divorce, I moved across the country to L.A., about 2000 miles away from my ex-wife. We decided to maintain our friendship and still talk once or twice a week. We had been on good terms, she had a boyfriend, and I was happy being "re-singled".

All the previous marital stress and frustration had long abated. We loved each other still, but had long realized we weren't ideal for each other.

All good, right?

That's what I thought. Little did I realize that even in this state of newfound happiness and relief for me, I still had not extricated myself fully from the old pain and old habits. In our attempt to be good friends who were honest with each other, we still found ourselves falling into old patterns. We still pushed each other's buttons unintentionally, and still overreacted to each other like we had when we were married. Despite the facts that we had not seen each other face-to-face in months, were 2000 miles apart, and were happier than we had been in years, we somehow were still angering each other to no end, crying heavily, and were generally living wrecks. The kicker is we hadn't even been talking.

We were chatting over an IM computer program.

That's how entangled we still were in each other's lives. A couple of friends of mine advised me to stop talking for a while. I did…for about a month or so. When my ex and I next talked on the phone, we were very apologetic, realized how we needed more space, and that we needed to alter our relationship even further. I wanted to get to that ideal place of "best friends" right off the bat. However, that was obviously unrealistic. What we should have done immediately was not talk for a month or two, but we were still trying to keep as much closeness as possible during the split.

A lot of times that just can't happen.

As it is, we are fine now, but we could have gotten to that place quicker if we had taken more space and time away once the separation occurred.

Point being, there are many different relationships, and none are exactly alike. But one of the commonalities is that everyone is human, and everyone needs to take time away to clear their heads and pay attention to themselves again. The more time, emotion, and energy invested in a relationship, the more time you need apart during a break. That's just the way it is.

5) What is your feeling regarding sex?

It's good times!

Oh, that's not what you meant. Well, besides the advice of taking precautions to be safe, I feel personally that it's **very** important to know your partner intimately in every way. You have to know your partner in *every* possible way if you're looking for a *lifelong* partner. But then again, some people may think sexual chemistry isn't a need for them.

That's fine. However, to me, sex is about more than just the physicality. It actually reveals a lot more to me. It is the easiest means of exchanging energy, and with myself being very sensitive to energies, I can feel what energy is there and what energy isn't. I can feel what energies click and which don't. I can feel the emotions involved, and the openness of my partner. Oftentimes I can "feel" what the potential goodness and the potential problems can be this way too.

But that's just me, and no, it's not the primary reason I engage in that activity either.

I do it 'cause it's fun!

Have I said that yet?

However, the other thing I feel **really** strongly about regarding the topic of sex regards safety. And I'm not talking about the kind you normally hear about—the contraception (although that's very important too). Preserving your safety physically **is** important. But the preservation of an individual emotionally and spiritually is quite often overlooked and is just as important as preserving one's physical safety. It truly alarms me how many youngsters have sex at an early age nowadays.

I get the feeling that a lot of parents, "knowing" that their kids will engage in sexual activity anyway, just talk to them about using condoms and other contraceptives and send them on their way. That may protect their bodies and early pregnancy possibilities, but do these parents give any thought to how early intercourse can stunt someone's emotional and spiritual growth? The younger one is, the less their chances of being emotionally and spiritually stable and mature. Young teenagers and pre-teens are typically not well-rounded individuals yet. They normally do not have a good handle on life.

(I could even argue that fact for some late teens and some adults 20 and above too)

At any rate, these young adults typically do not have the best idea of who they are yet, and are usually focused more on "fitting in" with others, as opposed to finding comfort within their own skin. (Attention on others as opposed to attention on self) Sexual activity can become like a drug ***very*** easily to these people, leading to a stunted personal growth, and promoting dependency on others. And most likely, these youngsters are having sex with others who are younger and/or aren't emotionally and spiritually mature yet too. So the sexual activity is primarily physical in these cases. There's nothing wrong with that per se. But as impressionable young adults, who may be developing some sort of dependency habit on others, or on superficial aspects of life (their looks), the value of sex on every level may be lost on them.

Meaning that sex may never be anything more than a fun, physical act to these people as they grow older. Many times that's a **best** case scenario. I know people who have become "abusive" with that power, or on the flipside become so dependent on the sexual act, that it's hard for them to develop fulfilling "wholistic" relationships with others.

I also know people who, ironically, just don't know how to "open up" conversationally or emotionally in their everyday lives, and live shielded by their own fear of emotions and what not. So, this habit permeates every aspect of life, not just the act of sex.

Sex is fun, it's life-affirming, and it's an amazing bonding experience. But it's also a big responsibility, physically as well as emotionally and spiritually. Even if you are mature enough to handle it on every level in every situation, your current partner may not be. Remember, it's the easiest way (and possibly the most fun way) to exchange energy. And thus, it's easy to become addicted to that energy.

 Once that happens, attention is no longer placed on the self, and I've already discussed how losing that can have detrimental consequences in your personal and relationship life so I won't rehash that now. Remember that, treat your partner and the act of sex with respect, and treat it as a responsibility. If you do follow those guidelines I don't see a problem with sex, no matter what stage of a relationship you do that in, be it a first or fifty-first date.

6) When do you know that you're ready to get married?

I know I sound like a broken record here, but again, everyone is different in this regard. I've known people who have gotten married within the first month of knowing each other, and decades later they are still together. I've also known others who knew each other for 3,4,5, years or more, then decided to get married…and then got divorced. (I'm one of them) There is no tried and true rule as far as time is concerned. I think if I *had* general timetable guidelines though, they would be: Wait at least a year from when you first start dating to get married.

And, if you're not 100% sure that your partner is a lifelong one after three years, then don't get married. Of course, these are just guidelines I formulated based on my studies of relationships. There are always exceptions to the rule. Only you and your partner can create the best timetable for yourselves. Everyone's different in this regard. The key is to take enough time for yourselves to see what the reality is going to be between you two when things are tough (but I'll get to that more in a second).

The divorce rate keeps getting higher primarily because life seems to be getting faster for each succeeding generation, and people apparently have less time than they used to in order to focus on their relationships. And biological clocks and external pressures just add to the problem. Many people feel the "need" to get married by a certain time, so they can have children by a certain time, and so on and so on. But we as a society take less time than we need to see the reality, simply because "we don't have enough time" to invest in the relationship. The lack of time to devote to our relationships may be real or imagined, but in many cases, we don't realize the importance of taking our time in our relationships. Hence, the rising divorce rate.

More important than the time test though is the distance test. Like I mentioned in the previous question, if you take time away from your partner for a month or so, you **really** get a sense of what your true bond is. By saying "time away" here though, I don't mean "taking a break" from your partner. Careers and other life decisions can force much of this time away, but they're great indicators of where a couple stands. You need to have faith during the process, and if the bond is strong, the relationship will sustain. That's a good sign. That's a great test of your bond. That's why I believe that any relationship that's meant to be will happen, no matter how much time is spent apart, and no matter how bad things may get at times. Again, it's all about the bond.

Both the time and distance tests are important in a way because they both are large factors in what I call the "Reality" test.

And the Reality test is the main test any couple should pass before declaring a lifelong commitment to each other. Relationship Law #12: *A couple needs to let reality hit to find out just how compatible they are.* This may take days, months, or years, depending on the individuals involved. But the reality must be seen. Each partner must be seen as exactly who they are, in good times and bad. Each partner must see how they can adjust to rough moments with each other.

Will each individual help the other through moments of crisis, or will they worsen the situation? Can they compromise? Can they work on their cooperative problem-solving? *It's the bad times that often determine the quality and longevity of a couple, not the good times.* Having more good times may make the duration more enjoyable, but it can also prolong the resolution of potential problems that may occur. I'm not saying that experiencing **more** bad times than good is the desired goal here, I'm only saying that you can learn **SO** much more about your relationship during the bad times than the good times. *The goal in relationships is to have mostly good times, but PRODUCTIVE bad times.*

When you know your partner inside and out, and know the exact reality of the situation, still are in love with your partner, still respect your partner as much as ever, and feel closer to them because of the reality, then you are ready for a lifelong commitment. (Is that enough for ya?) Time and distance are good indicators for the reality, but the biggest indicator is spending a lot of time and energy **with** them-- discovering who your partner is intimately in every way imaginable.

I know a lot of you may disagree with the following statement for varying reasons, but I believe it's really **smart** to actually live with someone before tying the knot. It may not be romantic, religious, or whatever, but it is logical. People always say, "Most relationships where people live together before getting married don't work out." I think this is one of the most absurd things I've ever heard. Aren't you *glad* that these people learned this situation didn't work **before** they got married? How is it advantageous to get married and **then** realize you have problems when you live together afterwards? "Well, it forces you to work out the problems." Not necessarily.

I do agree that most people give up on relationships quicker nowadays then they used to, but they'd give up quicker in marriage then too. This has **nothing** to do with whether they live together before or after they get married. And to those of you that say, "Well, living together is just like dating someone for two years who you spend a lot of time with". Umm…obviously you haven't lived with a partner before. Or you have a very boring, or fake, partner. Excuse my bluntness, but **no one** is exactly the same at their sanctuary 24-7 as they are when they are focused on you in a dating situation. And it's still different even if they sleep over every night, or they stay at your place for a week straight. I don't count it as truly "living together" until a couple has lived together at least a few months. You will never see your partner more selfish, petty, dull, moody, and just flat out weird as you will as when you live with them. "Why would I want to see that?" you ask. Because you supposedly want a real relationship (reality), and not a fantasy, right?

"No, I want a fantasy." Well, I hate to say it, but if that's your answer you'll never have a fulfilling lifelong relationship then. Even more so than the time and distance tests, living together is the single-most helpful thing you can do to determine the reality of your relationship situation.

Marriage is a wonderful ideal, but the truth is, many people who are married *shouldn't* be. It is a *huge* commitment, one that many aren't ready for. I wasn't ready for it when I was married, and there's no guarantee I ever will be. That's just who I am. But I realize that now, and know all of my needs a lot better now. I can promise you that if I do ever get married again, I will truly be ready the next time around.

Most people don't have any idea what getting married truly entails. It should be a wonderful continuation of a **great** couple who have an amazing bond, who love and respect each other very much, and who can solve any problems that may arise with minimal suffering. To those couples, marriage probably doesn't feel like much of an effort. That's great. But there are always problems that need to be addressed. Unfortunately, many married couples are **not** great couples. That's fine too, but whether or not those couples will work out is a bit of a riskier proposition. I personally think that if you do not qualify as a **great** couple, my advice is don't get married…at least not yet.

But no matter what kind of couple you are, you *do* have to work at it…some couples just more than others. If you *enjoy* the process and the journey most of the time, you're okay. When the suffering exceeds or matches the joy…that's a sign that the situation is not exactly the ideal relationship for you.

That's why at some point when the energy-high wears off, the "in-love" feeling relaxes, and the honeymoon is done in the early stages of the relationship, the most important phase of the relationship begins—the reality.

That's also why so many people leave the situation after a few months, because they don't want the responsibility of dealing with the reality. No, it's not always fun, and if you don't have your own life in order, how could you hope to help someone else with theirs? There's nothing necessarily wrong with that, as long as you're honest with yourself and your temporary partners about it. **KNOW WHO YOU ARE. KNOW WHAT YOUR RELATIONSHIP NEEDS ARE. KNOW WHAT YOUR RELATIONSHIP REALITY IS.** (See how the honesty is the common theme through this whole book?)

So spend time with your partner as much as possible, and when the time is right, you might want to move in together, even if it's just a temporary trial run for a few months or so. Reality will hit, but if you two can handle it well, you're in very good shape. And as a final test of your bond, take some time away from each other for a while. It's a sort of self-check you can't get while you are around your partner. If things still look good, and your bond still feels solid, then you're golden. Have a wonderful life together, I say!

FUNDAMENTALS REVISITED -ONE STEP AT A TIME-

I hope I didn't scare any of you **away** from relationships of the intimate kind! They are indeed wonderful. But they take effort and responsibility to do them right. Your gears *will* get squeaky from time to time, and will maybe even break. Most of us are ill-prepared for that, which is the reason I've written this book. Now you should have a solid grasp of what to focus on, and how to "oil your own gears".

Again, I know I haven't covered everything pertaining to relationships in this one book. If I did, this book would be over 10,000 pages long. Also, I would be quoting every author, counselor, or person who ever gave me any advice on relationships if I wrote a book that long. But that wasn't the focus here. This book was intended purely as *my* view of relationships. If you want to hear or read what other "Love and Relationship Experts" have to say, check out their books. Trust me, I won't be offended. I know that I am not the "Be All End All" of relationship advice, so please stay open to advice from others as well. Sometimes some of the best quotes I hear from anyone regarding relationships are from students at my shows! Everyone has something to teach. But this is my personal relationship philosophy which I'm sure can give all of you, at the very least, a solid foundation off which to work.

The cliffs notes version of my philosophy is as follows…refer to it if you ever need a quick reminder…

In summation, identify your personal needs first! Keep constant checks on those needs and take steps to fulfill them on your own. This will keep you happy. Remember, personal insecurities and unhappiness are the main factors that stand in the way of having a strong bond with another person. Next, identify your relationship needs and make sure you can have those needs filled by your partner somewhere along the line **before** you declare your relationship a lifelong one. At the very least, you must ensure that you have love, **respect**, trust, and communication in your relationship. Remember to ask "What do you need from me?" when you have problems, and learn to mirror for the more difficult times. The keys to all communication involve paying attention and listening. And finally, keep your relationship real and don't be afraid of that reality, for you **can** handle it.

If you do these things, you will have become, for all intents and purposes, a "whole" being. If you bring your whole being together with *another* whole being, the result is amazing beyond description. The only couples whom I would consider *great* ones are those with two *whole* people who have all of the qualities mentioned in the above paragraph.

And these people, unfortunately, are not in the majority.

There are a bunch of decent and good couples I know of, but honestly, I wouldn't be surprised if, as of this writing, they eventually split up. But quite a few of them, if they work on the relationship and pay it a good bit of attention, can eventually make the relationship a great one.

Remember nothing's set in stone. People after all *do* change. Because of this fact, there is quite a bit of faith in accepting someone as a life partner in marriage or some other form of long-term relationship. You never know what the future holds. That's why the fundamentals of friendship are so important. The passion will have its peaks and valleys, and honestly, the love will too. That's hard to maintain at *all* times. But you must hold on to the **respect** at all times. That's the key.

Also remember that many couples can be good together in good times. It's the *tough* times that truly show the character of the partners and the strength of the relationship. Hopefully now **you** can enjoy the good times, with no fear of the bad times, because you are now better prepared to deal with the obstacles. You know how to find the right relationship, and know how to take care of the problems that occur in one. Remember that even the best of relationships will have problems.

I don't know if you realize this, but these fundamentals I've written about can apply to just about **any** relationship you have: Friendships, familial relationships, business relationships, and even for dealing with strangers assuming you talk to them at all, of course. For example, if you need to mirror with a parent, or a good friend, the same rules apply. At work, if you're ever confused about your workload for the day, or are unsure of how to handle your boss, ask, "What do you need from me?" Beware of any yellow or red flags with any strangers you meet to make sure they meet **your** criteria for association. And of course, if you focus on yourself and your needs first, you'll be amazed how much easier all of this is to do.

Finally, here are my Relationship Gears and Laws to remember once more:

GEARS:
1) Labels don't matter, bonds do.
2) Happiness=Energy=Attention…give yourself attention for happiness.
3) Identify Your Needs~Individual Needs+ Love, Communication, and Respect
4) Be With A Best Friend—(and Respect, respect, respect)
5) Talk Through Your Crazy, And Listen Through Your Stupid-Keep Communication lines open.

LAWS:
1) Every relationship is different and unique.
2) YOU are all experts of your own life. No one knows you better than you.
3) Don't put the cart before the horse-the bond makes the label, not the other way around. Take your time to find the bond.
4) The less controlling the partners, the more the relationship can flourish.
5) You are not **truly** ready to be intimate with another person until you have a solid connection with yourself.
6) Depend on yourself for fulfilling your needs, not others. Depending on others is a sign of neediness. Neediness overrides all good intentions.
7) Rejection is a reflection of someone's needs…no more, no less.
8) You can compromise things that you want, NOT things that you need.
9) Healthy communication comes out of respect, and ease of communication comes out of personal happiness.

10) Men are stupid, women are crazy…seemingly so because the two sexes are geared differently.
11) Talking through your issues is ALWAYS better than holding things in.
12) A couple needs to let reality hit before they know exactly how compatible they are.
13) A strong bond leads to trust and faith. Relationships all need trust and faith.

That last law I have touched on throughout this book but haven't spelled out as a law until now, simply because I want you to remember that one the most as you end this book. **All** healthy relationships need trust and faith. You need to **trust** in your partner at all times, and that is created through a strong bond. But no matter how great you are with your partner now, you also have to have **faith** that the relationship will remain solid and even grow in time. Nothing is set in stone, things can always change. Don't let that scare you, for **everybody** is in the same boat.

Nobody can read their own future. Even those that say they can are basing that on faith. Remember, if you have that solid bond--and you should know exactly how to go about finding that now--and the trust is there, you have laid the best possible foundation you can have for a relationship. The rest is based on faith. You have to stay positive. That's the only other ground rule. That's the only way to let the bond survive, evolve, and flourish.

Have faith…in your partner, and most of all, yourself. You now have the tools, and know how to go about using them. Have faith in all of that. Remember these fundamentals! Be great! Good luck to you in every walk of life. Do self-checks! Do all of these things, and you have a great chance at "winning the relationship game." May you keep your love life in gear!

ACKNOWLEDGMENTS AND THANKYOUS

There are so many of you to thank, and only so much room to do it in! For many reasons throughout this book (such as protecting privacy), I will not use anyone's proper name. Plus, you guys should know who you are anyway, right? Right!

So here goes...

First and foremost, I'd like to thank my family--

My mom and dad...for teaching me everything that I consider important in life, such as how to deal with people, how to be happy as an individual apart from others, and of course, for providing a wonderful example of what a happy couple should be! You have been and always will be my loving anchor. I love you guys.

My sister...who spiritually is much older than I am, and therefore is the one person who constantly helps me put things in perspective, and who teaches me how to set boundaries. One day she SHOULD write a book called, "How to say NO!" Thank you for teaching me the value of that word. You are my best friend. I love you too.

Secondly, my friends, every single one of them…without you all I would not have learned so much, laughed so hard, and talked so endlessly! (to the relief of my sister, who keeps saying, "NO!" to my babbling to HER…so she too thanks you for your listening) Each and every one of you I have a special and unique bond with, and I wouldn't trade that for anything.

Thirdly, all of my "exes"…thank you for being so loving (in your own unique ways), helping me find my needs along the way, and for helping me evolve. I learned so much from you and love you all for those things…

Most importantly out of my exes, I would like to thank my ex-wife. Thank you for everything. Despite our issues during our time together, we still shared a lot of laughter, learned a lot about ourselves, and have evolved to the next level of our lives. I don't think I could have done this without you. All my thanks, and my love…

And last, but DEFINITELY not least, my current lady, who is the peak of my relationship pyramid. You challenge me, support me, and love me so much through all of my endeavors and my "unique ways." I hope you are still coping okay…) You are a true "teammate." You are amazing, and I think you fit me just right. I like our chances…I love you very much.

You have all influenced this book to one degree or another, and I thank you all for that. I hope you'll all enjoy it and don't get offended by it!

LoveG.E.A.R.S.

www.ingramcontent.com/pod-product-compliance
Lightning Source LLC
Chambersburg PA
CBHW071702040426
42446CB00011B/1874